Inspiring Growth and Leadership in Medical Careers

TRANSFORM HEALTHCARE AS A PHYSICIAN LEADER

Peter B. Angood, MD, FRCS(C), FACS, MCCM, FAAPL(Hon)

American Association for
PHYSICIAN
LEADERSHIP

PUBLISHER
Nancy Collins

PRODUCTION MANAGER
Jennifer Weiss

EDITOR
Hannah Irish

DESIGN & LAYOUT
Carter Publishing Studio

COVER PHOTO
Ida M. Covi, MA

TABLE OF CONTENTS

DEDICATION

Healthcare is a complex industry and, as such, it is ever in need of stronger leadership and better-defined future directions, at all levels. These efforts are for the sake of patients and their families, the primary beneficiaries of further improvements and more refined approaches to supporting health and delivering compassionate care. This book is dedicated to those already providing tangible, evident leadership at all levels in healthcare. Thank you for your efforts.

This book is also dedicated, perhaps more importantly, to those who will soon become future leaders in healthcare. Though this industry continues to challenge each of us, it remains an honor and privilege to help others manage their health or treat them when disease inevitably arrives to change their lives. Remember, leadership can occur at all levels, not just in formalized, titled roles within an institution. Embrace the opportunity to create larger scales of change for others.

ACKNOWLEDGMENTS

Nancy Collins continues to provide exceptional support, insights, and encouragement for the development and production of a full spectrum of information resources at the American Association for Physician Leadership (AAPL). Her own leadership talents are evident on a routine basis and it is with deep gratitude that I personally benefitted from her direction during the process of developing this book on leadership in healthcare. She is a tour de force — thank you!

Jennifer Weiss and Hannah Irish are also to be thanked for their contributions in the development and delivery of this book. Both are wonderful editors in their own rights and were highly effective with bringing this book to the light of day. Jen, your efficiencies and consistency are most appreciated. Hannah, your suggestions and thought processes were unique and discerning in a professional fashion not often witnessed in the publishing process. Thank you both for your contributions!

The leadership team at AAPL (Tony Talbot, Michelle Martin, Brian Fending), all the AAPL staff, and Sarah Cammer with the AAPL Board of Directors must each be acknowledged for their deep levels of commitment to augmenting leadership capabilities in healthcare, as well as for their ongoing contributions to AAPL as the association itself continues to make its mark on the industry as best as is possible. The quality and professionalism demonstrated on a daily basis is exceptional and a privilege to witness, as well as to learn from — thank you one and all!

Finally, our current (and future) AAPL constituency members need to be recognized for their ongoing commitment to patient care delivery and for their efforts to improve the overall health of our communities. It is the healthcare workforce who really are the leaders in this industry. The altruism, the idealism, and the everyday compassion so readily demonstrated to others are minor miracles not always appreciated. Please keep up your daily efforts and your persistent leadership. We all need you — thank you!

Signature

Dr. Peter B. Angood

About the Author

Peter B. Angood, MD, FRCS(C), FACS, MCCM, FAAPL(Hon)

 Peter Angood, MD, is currently CEO and president of the American Association for Physician Leadership. Previously, Dr. Angood was the inaugural chief patient safety officer at The Joint Commission, patient safety adviser to the World Health Organization (WHO), senior adviser for patient safety at the National Quality Forum, and chief medical officer for the Patient Safety Organization of GE Healthcare. Prior to this, he enjoyed 25 years of academic trauma surgery practice ranging from McGill University in Canada to the University of Pennsylvania, Yale University, and Washington University in St. Louis. Dr. Angood completed his academic career as a full professor of surgery, anesthesia, and emergency medicine. He remains actively involved with a variety of healthcare advisory groups and professional societies, has served as president for the Society of Critical Care Medicine, and is a well-recognized international speaker and author with 250 publications. His previous book, *All Physicians Are Leaders*, has been critically well received. The AAPL podcast, *Inspired Healthcare Leaders with Peter Angood, MD*, will debut in 2024.

pangood@physicianleaders.org

Physician Leadership — Always Being Watched

Several years ago, I was hosting an annual physician thought-leadership meeting, during which two intriguing and especially important moments occurred for me, both in relation to the honorary fellows being celebrated that year.

Dr. David Shulkin (then-U.S. Secretary of Veterans Affairs) spoke at a luncheon. His remarks on the Department of Veterans Affairs were poignant and insightful for the audience. I was also impressed when I saw how many attendees stood up when he called upon them to demonstrate the presence of veterans who had served within our community.

After Shulkin's remarks, while he informally interacted with the audience offstage, I spent a few minutes chatting with a member of his security detail. Turns out this gentleman was a longtime member of the federal security services and was married to a physician. He went on to describe his wife's clinical activity, but he also described how they both were feeling the pressures of current medical practice and its impact on their personal lives.

His story about the personal impact on an entire family was not too different from the stories many of us have. The conversation was an important reminder to me about how you never know who or when someone is paying attention to your work and the importance of physician leadership in society.

Dr. Ram Raju (then-senior vice president and community health investment officer at Northwell Health) spoke during a reception later that day. His comments were equally profound and concerned the critical importance of why our industry must better serve society's vulnerable populations. He clearly articulated the vital significance of why doing this well not only improves the lives of those affected but also improves how the institutions providing services and the financial payers all benefit with significantly better outcomes.

After the reception, a lead staff member of the venue approached me, stretching out his hand and thanking me for having witnessed Raju's address. The gentleman was almost in tears as he briefly explained how his family (and so many on his staff) struggled desperately with healthcare coverage, let alone how to live healthier lifestyles. Still, among all the meetings he witnesses, he had recognized the special nature and tone of ours — especially the focus on physician leadership and the efforts to improve the overall well-being of the industry.

Once more, I was reminded of the indirect influence physicians create when others are watching, and that we might not be aware of how our behaviors or actions are being absorbed. As physicians, we carry an important responsibility — always.

So, yes, we are always being watched at some level. At a minimum, our family and friends have been watching us since our early student days when it became evident to them that medicine was a career path. The hope, the envy, the admiration were all present in some fashion. As careers progress, the circumference of who is watching gradually expands – peer trainees, nurses, faculty, and others in the clinical arena. Then one's practice begins to get established and your credibility as a physician is monitored by patients, patient families, and office or hospital staff. Before you know it, a professional reputation has been established and impressions of your professional skill sets will become engrained in your community. Then it all keeps growing with escalating opportunities for broader community engagement in an assortment of ways.

And yet, others are always watching. This is the nature of being a physician. It therefore is also an opportunity to emulate the traits of being a leader in the community. You do not need formal titled roles and a load of administrative responsibility to be recognized as a leader. Our natural traits of altruism, commitment to others, and a desire to help create positive change on many levels are the attributes of leadership that will be recognized by others as they continue to watch.

The physician's position is an honor and a privilege to hold. Thus, be ever mindful that losing the confidence and trust of this audience is exceedingly tough to reverse.

SECTION ONE

Beginnings

CHAPTER 1

Culture and Communities of Practice in Changing Times

As we grow and age, we engage with or aspire to become a part of a multitude of cultures and communities. Do you have a current community or culture vital to your well-being and identity? Do you remember your initial awareness of culture or community?

Familial and ethnic cultural backgrounds are clearly important, but what I am considering here are the cultures and communities separate from our heritages that provide us with a place of learning, personal happiness, and individual character. For example, beyond medicine, I most often identify with the outdoors or athletic communities and the cultural habits within them. This manifests itself in the types of activities I learn, follow, or participate in and includes the style or brands of clothing and equipment I purchase. And I must say there is way too much equipment in my gear closet nowadays as a result. But that story is for another day . . .

The medical profession is both a culture and a community of practice, and within our profession, there are numerous sub-cultures and unique communities of practice. The recent pandemic has significantly shifted our culture, our profession, our industry, and our communities of practice. Similarly, the non-medical society has shifted its view of healthcare and its expectations for receiving optimal care. How we now adapt and change is foundational for future directions of physician leadership.

According to Nicki Lisa Cole, PhD,[1] the term "culture" refers to "a large and diverse set of mostly intangible aspects of social life," and it is "composed of both non-material and material things." Sociologists define the non-material aspects of culture as "the values and beliefs, language, communication, and practices that are shared in common by a group of people," while "Material culture is composed of the things that humans make and use. This aspect of culture includes a wide variety of things, from buildings, technological gadgets, and clothing, to film, music, literature, and art, among others."

Due to its crucial role in social life, Cole states that sociologists recognize culture as one of sociology's most important concepts: "It is important for shaping social relationships, maintaining and challenging social order, determining how we make sense of the world and our place in it, and in shaping our everyday actions and experiences in society." Cole further explains that culture is important to sociologists because it plays a significant role in the production of social order, which refers to "the stability of society based on the collective agreement to rules and norms that allow us to cooperate, function as a society, and live together (ideally) in peace and harmony." Additionally, while culture is distinct from social structure and economics, "it is connected to them—both continuously informing them and being informed by them."

Relatedly, a community is a social group whose members have something in common, such as a shared government, geographic location, culture, or heritage. More generally, according to Dictionary.com, community can refer to a group that shares some trait or quality that separates it from the wider population. A "community of practice," however, is described by social theorists Etienne and Beverly Wenger-Trayner[2] as a group of people who share a concern or a passion for something they do and learn how to do it better as they interact regularly. These communities have been around for as long as human beings have learned together. They explain, "at home, at work, at school, and through hobbies, we all belong to communities of practice. In some, we are core members, but in many we are merely peripheral. And we participate with numerous communities over the course of our lives."

Anthropologists Jean Lave and Etienne Wenger-Trayner coined the term "community of practice" while studying apprenticeship as a learning model. People usually think of apprenticeship as a relationship between a student and a master, but studies of apprenticeship reveal a more complex set of social relationships through which learning takes place, mostly with journeymen and more advanced apprentices. Think initially of how your own medical school and residency training programs were similar.

The concept of a community of practice has found several practical applications in business, organizational design, government, education, professional associations, development projects, and civic life. Communities of practice are everywhere. They are a familiar experience — so familiar, perhaps, that they often escape our attention. Yet when given a name and brought into focus, a community of practice becomes a perspective that can help us better understand our world. It allows us to see past more obvious formal structures, such as organizations, classrooms, or nations, and perceive the structures defined by engagement in practice and the informal learning that comes with it.

The Wenger-Trayners describe three crucial characteristics, and state it is their combination that constitutes a community of practice:

The domain. A community of practice is not merely a club of friends or a network of connections between people. It has an identity defined by a shared domain of interest. Membership implies a commitment to the domain and, therefore, a shared competence that distinguishes members from other people.

The community. In pursuing their interest in their domain, members engage in joint activities and discussions, help each other, and share information. They build relationships that enable them to learn from each other; they care about their standing with each other.

The practice. A community of practice is not merely a community of interest — people who like certain kinds of movies, for instance. Members of a community of practice are practitioners. They develop a shared repertoire of resources: experiences, stories, tools, ways of addressing recurring problems — in short, a shared practice.

Now consider how this concept influences your own approach to ongoing clinical skills acumen, as well as your unique approaches toward physician leadership development. Consider, also, the many evolving differences in the way our healthcare industry views its cultures, as well as the communities of practice in which we reside, including workforce migrations and shifting levels of commitment or loyalties toward patient care, for example. Patients themselves have varying expectations for their healthcare, and our payment system continues to create hurdles for all-inclusive care as we attempt to embrace the nuances for social determinants of health. And the list could go on and on . . .

Embracing change is always important, and physician leadership has the opportunity to reshape these evolving healthcare cultures. It is indeed an exciting time for creating potentially significant shifts in healthcare!

REFERENCES

1. Cole NL. So What Is Culture, Exactly? *ThoughtCo*. August 1, 2019. https://www.thoughtco.com/culture-definition-4135409
2. Wenger-Trayner E, Wenger-Trayner B. Introduction to Communities of Practice. be@wenger-trayner.com.

CHAPTER 2

Kindness, Goodness, and Gratitude — Food for Our Spirits

Most of us have heard of or seen the bumper sticker "Practice Random Acts of Kindness." And yet, when was the last time any of us followed that direction outside of our professional environments?

I was young, maybe 12 or so, when I watched an older man stop to help a seemingly homeless woman who had been beaten and was lying still on the street. He gently shook the woman to see if she was alive, and when he got a response, asked her how he might help. He propped her up against the side of a building, organized her clothing to be more comfortable, and called 911.

He waited with her, softly assuring her that help was on the way. As the ambulance team arrived and began their assessments, he remained at her side, holding her hand while they loaded her onto the gurney. The man reassured the woman that she would soon be in a place where others would help her, then spoke directly to the EMTs, conveying that he expected them to treat her with respect and kindness. The ambulance left, and he walked away without acknowledging the gathered crowd.

Whenever I remember that event or see that bumper sticker, I am reminded to practice those random acts of kindness. What act of kindness inspired you and changed your behavior?

Being kind to others and to yourself has many positive benefits. Kindness increases self-esteem, empathy, and compassion, and improves our mood. It can decrease blood pressure and stress hormones while boosting serotonin and dopamine, which affect stress levels. People who give of themselves in a balanced way also tend to be healthier and live longer. Kindness can increase our sense of connectivity with others, which can dispel feelings of loneliness, improve depression, and enhance relationships in general.

Unfortunately, recent Medscape Burnout Survey results show frustratingly high numbers (see Figure 1). In 2021, 42% of physicians expressed feelings of burnout; in 2022, the percentage increased to 47%. Gender differences were significant, with a 56% rate of burnout for women and 41% for men.

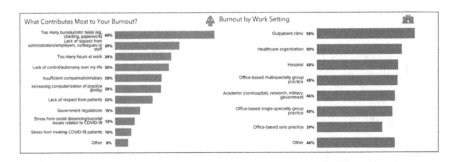

FIGURE 1. Contributions to Physician Burnout and Burnout by Work Setting

The COVID-19 pandemic likely contributed to these recent burnout rates. Individuals in other industries also experienced higher than usual rates of anxiety, burnout, and stress. This presents an interesting paradox for the physician workforce — the providers of care for others.

Additionally, physicians are notoriously resistant to seeking mental health assistance (see Figure 2). We believe, and our profession has perpetuated the belief, that physicians should not demonstrate "weakness" and should be a "strength figure" for the communities where we practice. Fortunately, this is gradually changing within the profession as society recognizes that mental health should be acknowledged and managed. High-profile individuals speaking out on mental health has certainly helped in this regard.

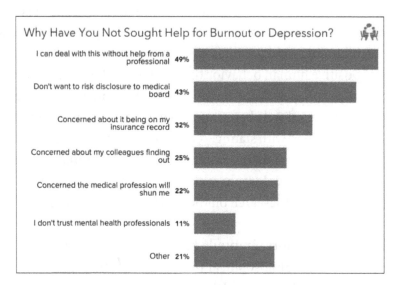

FIGURE 2. Physicians' Stated Reasons for Not Seeking Help for Burnout or Depression

With this intrinsic resistance to seeking out advice or assistance, we as physicians should reach out to one another more often to provide mutually beneficial peer-to-peer kindness and support. Who better understands? A simple act of goodness to another physician could have profound effects.

Mark Greenawald is one physician who recently started such an approach with an initiative called PeerRxMed™. As stated on the website, "PeerRxMed™ is a free, peer-supported program designed to help physicians and others on the care team move toward thriving both personally and professionally."[1] It is an interesting approach.

Confucius said, "True goodness springs from a man's own heart. All men are born good. Without goodness one cannot enjoy enduring happiness." Goodness is a virtue often thought to be an inherent characteristic of humans. It strongly relates to kindness, generosity, and a humane approach to life. Goodness is a positive, loving, and caring attitude revealed through our emotions and character. Being good is often thought to mean making life an enjoyable and satisfying experience for ourselves and others through moral, responsible choices.

Well, if kindness and goodness are outwardly expressed characteristics of positive human behavior that lead to a better life, how about an inwardly expressed characteristic that adds positive value in terms of improved mental well-being and a balanced approach to life?

Cicero is credited with stating, "Gratitude is not only the greatest of the virtues, but the parent of all of the others." In "Gratitude — Parent of All Virtues," Wood, Joseph, and Linley explore the concepts and then-current state of research on the topic of gratitude. Some of their concepts follow:[2]

- "Throughout history, gratitude has been given a central position in religious and philosophical theories. . . . including Buddhism, Christianity, Judaism, and Islam. . . . From a secular perspective, Adam Smith . . . . believed that gratitude was essential for society, motivating reciprocation of aid when no other legal or economic incentive encouraged its repayment."

- "Gratitude can be conceptualized as an affect, a behavior, or a personality trait . . . . Specifically, it acts as a moral barometer, drawing attention to help received; a moral motivator, encouraging a prosocial response to help; and as a moral reinforcer, where the expression of gratitude makes the benefactor more likely to provide help in the future."

- "Most recent research has focused on gratitude as a personality characteristic. Some people feel much more gratitude than others, reporting gratitude, which is more frequent, more intense, and involves appreciation of a wider range of people and events. . . . Multiple studies suggest that people who feel more gratitude are much more likely to have higher levels of happiness, and lower levels of depression and stress."

- As a personality trait, gratitude "... seems to have one of the strongest links with mental health of any personality variable. ... [and] may be uniquely important in social relationships. The 'moral' effects of emotional gratitude are likely to be as important in maintaining individual relationships as in maintaining a smooth-running society. People who feel more gratitude in life should be more likely to notice they have been helped, respond appropriately, and return the help at some future time."

- "Empirical evidence is fast accumulating that gratitude is involved in various social processes and is an important part of mental health and well-being. Such evidence is fully consistent with traditional treatments of gratitude by theologians and philosophers."

Similarly, it has been noted in several popular psychology articles that the simple act of keeping a daily gratitude journal helps us better appreciate our lives and may offer a path toward feeling more successful. Gratitude has been around since ancient times but is now being better recognized on several levels to benefit personal health and balance in our lives. Given the levels of burnout and its causes, perhaps seeking ways to find more gratitude in our lives will help brighten even those darkest of days and moments of highest frustration.

Be assured, however, that I am not suggesting that simple acts of kindness, goodness, or gratitude will solve the complex issues related to anxiety, burnout, and suicidality in healthcare. Large-scale systems change is required in healthcare before the workforce can step back and recognize things are indeed better. But we all need to engage in creating that change as best we can. There is no effort small enough to ignore when thinking of how to change our complicated industry. As physicians and physician leaders, we all need to help create the needed change and improvements. This collaboration to create change is, in my mind, a requirement for success in the next iteration of healthcare.

In the interim, sustaining a defense against the stresses and symptoms of burnout will be difficult at the best of times. Exhibiting kindness, demonstrating goodness, and being grateful for all the positive things in our lives will improve life for our families, friends, patients, peers, and ourselves!

Oh, and that man who helped the beaten woman? I learned later, by coincidence, he was the CEO of a large corporation. He followed up with her and eventually provided her a job at his company where she could get her life back on track.

It does not matter what station in life we are living; we can always be kind to others through acts of goodness. And we do not necessarily need to be told by others how kind or good we are. Being grateful that we have had the opportunity to be kind or good is reward enough!

REFERENCES

1. Greenawald M. *PeerRxMed*™. https://www.peerrxmed.com. Accessed November 26, 2023.
2. Wood A, Joseph S, Linley A. Gratitude — Parent of all virtues. *The British Psychological Society*. January 20, 2007. https://thepsychologist.bps.org .uk/volume-20/edition-1/gratitude-parent-all-virtues. Accessed November 26, 2023.

CHAPTER 3

The Only Constant is Change

We all hear it these days — ". . . healthcare is undergoing profound change, and we need to be ready." This phrase has been circulating for the better part of our careers. I graduated from medical school in 1981 and remember hearing about the needed changes for healthcare. I also remember commenting to a senior faculty person while I was a surgery resident about how I thought his generation had it better than our coming generation. Interestingly, his immediate response was, "Actually, Peter, I think the generation before mine had it perfectly." Over the years there have been numerous other examples for me as well.

Physicians care deeply about patients and people in general. We proudly wear our altruism and idealism on our sleeves. And, yes, at times, the grass can be greener elsewhere. But in our drive toward greener grass, we continually seek ways to better manage or control our environments. This is often an inherent component of physician personalities. Sometimes we succeed in our efforts with managing the circumstances, while at other times we become frustrated and even demoralized. Nonetheless, doing what is best for patients remains a core belief and an essential beacon of stability in healthcare. From my perspective, students and trainees of today continue with that same sense of value — perhaps even stronger than prior generations.

The paradox is this, however: human beings are human beings, and our core physiological, biochemical, and biological processes do not change that drastically over relatively short periods of time. Yes, the general health and welfare of people gradually change, and the evolution of disease states also gradually change over time. But none

13

of those changes are rapid, and it takes decades, generations, or even centuries for the changes to become evident. Human beings are, after all, human beings.

So where is all the change coming from? A short list includes:

- Improved basic understanding of our biology and physiology.
- Development of better pharmaceuticals and medical devices.
- An appreciation that focusing on preventive health may be a preferred approach to managing disease states.
- Recognition that supporting sciences such as epidemiology and biostatistics can refine our understandings.
- The realization that implementing a continuum-of-care approach will provide improved health and better patient outcomes.

The potentially more frustrating arenas of change for physicians, however, are not those related to the historical approaches for improving the science of medicine. They are changes imposed on the delivery of care because of:

- Increasing presence of political and policy engagement with healthcare.
- Escalating regulatory and oversight burdens.
- Expanding sets of inexact measures and flawed reporting efforts.
- Routine shifting of risk management and expense burdens.
- Ongoing uncertainty with the legal environment and future approaches within healthcare.
- Poorly aligned financial models that routinely confuse all participants in the industry.

Again, this is just a short list. While the evolution of human beings and disease states are slower, the exciting pace of change with science and technology continues to rapidly gain momentum at unprecedented levels. But it is the speed of change, the courses of change in healthcare delivery models, and the rapidly shifting policy, financial, or legal reform approaches that I hear about from fellow physicians.

The frustration with these changes is difficult to manage because these are areas in which physicians are not routinely provided the background education or opportunity to easily gain further knowledge and understanding.

When not able to understand, physicians can become discouraged by change. There is no inherent resistance to change itself, but more to the difficulty in knowing how to adapt and adjust to change when the circumstances or the environment are uncertain and unpredictable. In reality, physicians often are proud of the ability to flex, change, and innovate.

We are indeed in a state of perpetual change for the industry. But this is a critically important period in healthcare because it is being recognized and appreciated that physician leadership is pivotal for driving successful change in healthcare at all levels. I remain quite impressed with how the physician work force has become more engaged with learning how to adjust and participate constructively with these changes. Physicians are making significant impacts across a host of environments. Positive change is happening as a result of physician engagement.

CHAPTER 4

Adversity, Resilience, and Persistence

I enjoy endurance sports and spending time outdoors in difficult environments. I remember one day, for example, I was out running in the woods on muddy, puddle-laden trails in pouring rain. Part way through, I tripped, fell into a pool of murky water, and emerged completely covered in black ooze. After realizing I had no injury, I laughed at the situation for what I must have looked like and then carried on to complete what turned out to be a great run. I enjoyed it! This was not the first time I tripped on the trails, nor will it be the last. But why do I persist?

Certainly, I enjoy the physical benefits of lifelong fitness, but I also find that I relish that sense of accomplishment when something complex has been achieved. For me, it is often less about the journey and more about the result. Do not get me wrong here, though — although the results give me greater pleasure, the journey in these settings can also be deeply satisfying despite arduous and difficult circumstances.

Over time, I have benefited greatly by having my capabilities challenged by managing the difficulties of a journey and by learning to continually improve my approaches (mostly psychological). Those capabilities have improved because of my recognition that, when properly channeled, adversity inevitably will result in improved resilience. This, in turn, enables me with an improved ability to persist as I strive to reach my goals.

ADVERSITY

The *Merriam-Webster Dictionary* definition of adversity (noun) is: a difficult situation or condition; a misfortune or tragedy.

> "The most beautiful people we have known are those who have known defeat, known suffering, known struggle, known loss, and have found their way out of the depths. These persons have an appreciation, a sensitivity, and an understanding of life that fills them with compassion, gentleness, and a deep loving concern. Beautiful people do not just happen."
>
> — ELISABETH KÜBLER-ROSS
> Author. Well-recognized for 5 Stages of Grieving

Being physician leaders, we routinely face adversity — both professional and personal. We see numerous clinical examples daily, and we also see frequent examples of ways to manage it. The core nature of who we are as physicians, how we were trained, and how we practice our skills help provide us with the resilience to weather adversity.

RESILIENCE

The *Merriam-Webster Dictionary* definition of resilience (noun) is: able to become strong, healthy or successful again after something bad happens.

> "Resilient people do not let adversity define them. They find resilience by moving toward a goal beyond themselves, transcending pain and grief by perceiving bad times as a temporary state of affairs . . . It's possible to strengthen your inner self and your belief in yourself, to define yourself as capable and competent. It's possible to fortify your psyche. It's possible to develop a sense of mastery."
>
> — HARA ESTROFF MARANO
> Editor-at-Large for *Psychology Today*

Our long years of medical education require resilience! And then our persistence through that education prepares us to launch into a career trajectory that also requires ongoing resilience and persistence. Likely, most of us did not even recognize that we started to develop these critically important capabilities early in our careers. Turns out, it is a prescient set of skills.

As the healthcare industry continues to gain complexity and evolve at an ever-increasing pace, it is now almost imperative that if we do not already have natural resiliency, then we should each seek ways to gain it.

Almost all the adversities we witness in healthcare will continue in some fashion, and our need for persistence endures. Nonetheless, it is our personal resilience that will allow us to manage adversity better and use persistence to achieve better results.

PERSISTENCE

The *Merriam-Webster Dictionary* definition of persistence (noun) is: the quality that allows someone to continue doing something or trying to do something even though it is difficult or opposed by other people.

During World War II, well before my time, Winston Churchill tried to lift the spirits of the British people through an analogy for persistence. Knowing their ongoing fight with Germany was difficult, he painted the picture by saying, "The nose of the bulldog has been slanted backward so he can breathe without letting go (of his adversary)." From what I understand, this was a well-accepted and highly motivational moment for the British public and the armed forces.

While writing this chapter, I also came across a clinically relevant article that provided deeper insight into the thinking of the International Society for Pharmacoeconomics and Outcomes Research Medication Compliance and Persistence Work Group — a group that developed clinical definitions for compliance and persistence during three years of international review and discussion.

"Clinical outcomes of treatment are affected not only by how well patients take their medications, but also by how long they take their medications. Thus, compliance and persistence should be defined and measured separately to characterize medication-taking behavior comprehensively. Addressing both compliance and persistence provides a richer understanding of medication-taking behavior."[1]

I found this latter nuance intriguing, and it has placed the simple act of patient engagement in a much clearer context for me, personally. Certainly, our patients require resilience for general health approaches and in all types of treatment strategies for illness.

For them, these represent adversity and they will each make personal choices on their eventual compliance with the recommended approaches. But, regardless, persistence is always needed because that is the nature of illness and disease — adverse situations usually do not just go away. Positive or negative results will prevail, depending on the success of the treatment.

As physician leaders, we have to continually develop these complex skills of resilience and persistence; not only as individuals, but also for our patients and the organizations in which we work. All physicians are viewed as leaders at some level, and often the presumption is that innately we already have the ability to manage adversity effectively.

That is not always the case and it underscores my point on the need for each of us to consider how to evaluate our existing degree of resilience and how to expand it. Our persistence in improving resilience will not only provide a better end result for our patients and our organizations, but also will benefit ourselves, our families, and our circle of friends.

The story of Dr. Bennet Omalu is an intriguing story of exceptional success in taking on adversity with resilience and persistence. His early efforts in the past dozen years to define chronic traumatic encephalopathy in National Football League (NFL) players are continuing to be felt within professional sports around the globe.

In addition, there is now a recognition of potential head injuries within the general public, and this fact is dramatically changing the nature of organized amateur sports. For me, his story is not just about the NFL, but is one of scientific integrity that carries profound public health ramifications. By demonstrating personal resilience and effective persistence, Omalu overcame significant adversity to create a highly important end-result for society.

Physician leaders can learn a lot from stories about overcoming adversity. Physicians also can learn significantly from those highly motivated individuals we come across in the clinical delivery system — patients and providers.

We can all work toward creating large-scale change for healthcare by demonstrating resilience and persistence when it comes to improving the outcomes of patient care, and the outcomes for higher quality, safe, efficient systems of care. Our society benefits from the focus and skills of physicians when they serve as leaders. It is my core altruism and my personal commitment to physician leadership that help drive me to improve my own resilience. I do this by seeking a variety of challenges, which represent adversity, and they help me grow through my persistence. So if you see a muddy-looking trail runner approach, please do not turn away — laugh with them and let them know you appreciate what is going on under their mud-covered clothing. I encourage you to find your own version of the muddy trails and enjoy what it brings to your ongoing personal growth.

REFERENCE

1. Cramer JA, Roy A, Burrell A, et al. Medication compliance and persistence: terminology and definitions. www.ispor.org/heor-resources/good-practices-for-outcomes-research/article/medication-compliance-and-persistence-terminology-and-definitions.

CHAPTER 5

We Know About Physician Burnout; What About Physician Happiness?

I often mention this phrase because whether one pursues recognized leadership tracks or follows a career without formal leadership roles, those who enter the medical profession generally possess several natural leadership attributes, such as:

- Intelligence;
- Altruism;
- Ambition;
- Motivation;
- Empathy;
- Adaptability;
- Integrity; and
- Decisiveness.

In addition, most all societies continue to expect that physicians display leadership traits, both clinically and in nonclinical life.

While physician leadership had recently become somewhat marginalized within the industry, with the recent flux in healthcare we now see physician leadership regaining significant recognition. Trends such as the integration of physicians as salaried employees in health systems, the emphasis on outcomes-based payment models, and the need to drive clinical care using evidence-based protocols have created a growing demand for dedicated physician leadership. There is also an increase in physicians pursuing nontraditional career paths who seek advanced education and leadership training.

In the mission to support physician leaders, we continue to learn much about physician dissatisfaction. But, unfortunately, we do not yet hear much about physician happiness, wellness, or career satisfaction. While burnout concerns are important and relevant, we must also begin to refocus ourselves and our profession toward the positive aspects of being a physician and reconnect with an improved appreciation for the profound benefits achievable with this career.

At the very least, we not only owe it to ourselves as individuals, but we also owe something to those entering the profession. The quality of medical student applications remains at very high levels as our profession continues to draw the "best of the best."

To help maintain the appeal of this profession to potential physicians, it is our collective responsibility to begin fostering an improved image of the physician career path as an opportunity for someone to become a satisfied, well-adjusted individual. There are certainly a multitude of pressures, and we must continue to recognize and prevent or manage physician burnout. But it is also time to bring attention to achieving physician wellness, happiness, and balanced lives.

As highlighted in a recent Shannon article, "Physician Well-being: A Powerful Way to Improve the Patient Experience," the five domains that predict physician dissatisfaction and the contributions to burnout identified in the Minimizing Error, Maximizing Outcome (MEMO) study are worth paying attention to so we can reflect on how they are impacting our lives.[1] More importantly perhaps, we should also consider how we can modify these influences so that we can turn negative impacts into positive outcomes.

Dissatisfaction domains:

1. Income
2. Relationships

3. Autonomy
4. Practice environment
5. Broader market environment

Contributions to burnout from MEMO study:

1. Time pressure
2. Work control
3. Work pace
4. Values alignment

Are physicians really that different from other professionals? Every profession has its stressors, and clearly those who make their livelihood outside of the professions have a host of stressors as well. And all people need to work hard if they want to succeed in our increasingly complex society. For everyone, the current global societal shifts can be complex enough by themselves. Comparatively speaking, perhaps physicians have just as many stressors as others.

And yet, there are some relatively unique aspects that differentiate our profession, including the protracted education tracks and the length of time it takes before physicians are established in their careers after formal training. When you add in the stress of simultaneously trying to get a personal life off the ground, it is easy to see how a combination of these factors could potentially tip the balance unfavorably. Additionally, the deeply personal nature of caring for people creates unique responsibilities and higher levels of emotional stress when compared with other professions.

The steep trajectory and intensity at the beginning of physicians' careers often delays the opportunity for individual leadership skills to shine. As physicians progress through other career stages, those natural leadership aptitudes may actually continue to be suppressed if the balance has been shifted to the negative side of the satisfaction/dissatisfaction equation. For me, the importance of finding how physicians can regain that balance — or better yet, proactively keep their balance — is an absolute necessity, not only for individuals but also for our profession as a whole.

We all ultimately aspire to personal happiness, however it is defined. As physicians and leaders in society, we have the potential to better demonstrate how we can take important steps to achieve that happiness. Personal happiness can also be like an infectious disease. As an individual you will affect not only your own life, but your family's life, your patients' lives, and all those around you. This is one type of infection we should learn better how to replicate, not eradicate.

REFERENCE

1. Shannon D. Physician well-being: a powerful way to improve the patient experience. *Physician Exec.* May/June 2013;39(4):6-8,10,12.

Knowledge of Healthcare Environment

CHAPTER 6

Is Healthcare Upside Down?

As I originally wrote this in December of 2017, a major merger was announced that caught my attention and caused a shake of my head — a major pharmacy chain was buying a major health insurance company. It is common knowledge that merger/acquisition activity in the healthcare industry has been at an all-time high. And while I am not generally an alarmist, nor politically motivated in my commentaries, this particular acquisition, from my perspective, seemed to be different from what I would have expected. A reverse order of acquisition, if you will.

According to language of the news release: "CVS Health, a company at the forefront of changing the healthcare landscape, and Aetna, one of the nation's leading diversified healthcare benefits companies, announce the execution of a definitive merger agreement under which CVS Health will acquire all outstanding shares of Aetna. . . . This transaction fills an unmet need in the current healthcare system and presents a unique opportunity to redefine access to high-quality care in lower cost, local settings whether in the community, at home, or through digital tools. . . . This is a natural evolution for both companies as they seek to put the consumer at the center of healthcare delivery. CVS Health has steadily become an integrated healthcare company, and Aetna has moved beyond being a traditional insurer to focus more on consumer well-being."[1] The language of the announcement initially sounds altruistic and seemingly patient-centered — but is it? As you reread the statement, you will recognize there is only mention of consumers, and not patients.

CVS Health President and Chief Executive Officer Larry J. Merlo further stated: "This combination brings together the expertise of two great companies to remake the consumer healthcare experience. . . . We look forward to working with the talented people at Aetna to position the combined company as America's front door to quality healthcare, integrating more closely the work of doctors, pharmacists, other healthcare professionals and health benefits companies to create a platform that is easier to use and less expensive for consumers."[1] In the same release, comments from Aetna CEO Mark Bertolini were similarly oriented to consumers. Another phrase from the release stated: ". . . capabilities developed following this transaction will directly benefit clients of both companies and enable them to better manage their healthcare costs." Again, no patients, or even people, are mentioned in these phrases.

To be fair, there is a segment in the news release that occasionally mentions the word "patient" when describing "benefits for consumers," but the preponderance of language is focused on the financial aspects of the deal and "benefits to shareholders." As I delved deeper into the news of this acquisition, I noticed even the rhetorical language used within the descriptions of their respective companies (*see Table 1*) created another moment of pause in my thinking.

Certainly, the sheer size of these companies alone is able to create significant influence, but is it the correct influence? How far have we drifted as an industry from physician leadership as the primary driver for patient-centered care? And with this example of the free market at work, have we become upside down in our thinking on where the influences for patient-centered care are best generated?

upside down (adj.)[2] — A situation in which one owes more on a loan used to pay for an asset than that asset's current market value . . . . Negative equity is most common after the burst of an asset bubble. One with negative equity is said to be upside down in the loan.

TABLE 1. Corporate Boilerplate

CVS HEALTH
CVS Health is a pharmacy innovation company helping people on their path to better health. Through its 9,700 retail locations, more than 1,100 walk-in medical clinics, a leading pharmacy benefits manager with nearly 90 million plan members, a dedicated senior pharmacy care business serving more than one million patients per year, expanding specialty pharmacy services, and a leading stand-alone Medicare Part D prescription drug plan, the company enables people, businesses and communities to manage health in more affordable and effective ways. *(Source:* cvshealth.com*)*
AETNA
Aetna is one of the nation's leading diversified healthcare benefits companies, serving an estimated 44.6 million, at September 30, 2017, people with information and resources to help them make better informed decisions about their healthcare. Aetna offers a broad range of traditional, voluntary and consumer-directed health insurance products and related services, including medical, pharmacy, dental, behavioral health, group life and disability plans, and medical management capabilities, Medicaid healthcare management services, workers' compensation administrative services and health information technology products and services. *(Source:* aetna.com*)*

Drawing a comparison between being upside down in the financial markets and the physician workforce's influence on patient-centered care might be a stretch, but the fundamental concept is not far off. Doing what is best for patients, and doing so in a caring, compassionate fashion with open communication, is what physicians value as a highest priority. This value also is a core asset within healthcare.

I do not believe the asset bubble of physician leadership in healthcare, nor the attendant physician influence on patient-centered care, has (or is about to) burst. In fact, I believe strongly that the opposite is the scenario we are facing, that there is an ongoing demand in the marketplace for strong physician leadership.

Yes, mergers/acquisitions such as CVS-Aetna will catch our attention. But, still, there was language in the news release excerpts quoted in this column that asserts the importance of physicians.

As stated, the deal ". . . positions the combined company as America's front door to quality healthcare, integrating more closely the work of doctors, pharmacists, other healthcare professionals . . . ." The recognition that physicians, working in an interprofessional, team-based environment, potentially can come together in a new platform represented by this acquisition is intriguing. But only time will reveal the successes or failures of the new company — and its influence on healthcare delivery.

The critical issue in my mind is that we all continue to promulgate the importance of physician leadership — at all levels of the delivery system — and that we also continue to work closely with the various sectors of our industry to further promote the benefits of patient-centered care and shared decision-making with patients. If we do not continue to pursue this aspect of healthcare, then we run the risk that the dominant influences on true patient-centered care will gradually slip from the purview of physicians and other concerned clinical disciplines. A net result is that our industry becomes further upside down with its priorities, the messages become convoluted, and our clinical workforce becomes more disgruntled with an eroding influence in light of decreasing clarity of purpose.

Our clinical workforces already struggle enough as it is with anxieties, frustration, and burnout that often are related to the complexity of delivery systems. Beyond addressing the issues related to workforce fatigue, system complexity, and eventual burnout, being able to help our workforces remain focused toward a higher purpose will help support better morale as well. As physicians, we must continually seek how to optimize patient-centered care in the face of ever-increasing complexity. Providing this ongoing focus on the essential components of the industry is an important endeavor for us all as we continually help others to achieve improved professional satisfaction.

REFERENCES

1. CVS Health to Acquire Aetna. *CVSHealth*. December 3, 2017. https://www.cvshealth. com/news/company-news/cvs-health-to-acquire-aetna-combination-to-provide-consumers-wit.html.

2. Negative equity. *The Free Dictionary,* https://financial-dictionary.thefreedictionary. com/upside+down. Accessed November 13, 2023.

CHAPTER 7

Redefining a Value Equation with Physicians as Leaders

Although physicians continue to provide, or directly supervise, almost 95% of patient care, they are not necessarily the pivot point around which healthcare is being redesigned or delivered for the future. The historical value of physicians and their leadership in healthcare is not guaranteed or assured.

Most of us know the value equation as Value = Quality/Cost. But do we truly understand and fully appreciate the value of physician leadership?

Historically, healthcare revolved around the knowledge and decision-making of physicians. The Flexner Report and its related consequences from the early 1900s have now driven the orientation of healthcare education and clinical delivery strategies in profound fashion for more than 100 years. Being able to move beyond these legacy behaviors is recognized as complex, and it will take several more years before we can look back and note that significant change has occurred.

Also coming into play is the fact that our industry has several competing agendas gradually evolving. Shifting clinical delivery models, new financial payment models, multi-professional team-based care, changing continuing medical education platforms, and a continual flow of new policy initiatives are among the developments. Additionally, the non-physician clinical disciplines are evolving in their own approaches on how to contribute in new ways to patient care.

Paul Keckley, PhD, a renowned healthcare economist assisted me with a survey on clarifying the issues physician leaders face and how they achieve success. This includes the issues for physicians in informal leadership roles as well as those in titled positions.

Highlights of a recent American Association for Physician Leadership (AAPL) member survey showed that 55% of respondents said they agreed or strongly agreed that the Affordable Care Act, passed in 2010, had "more good than bad" in it. In addition:

- 69% of respondents agreed or strongly agreed that physicians should be held accountable for costs of care in addition to quality of care.
- 57% of respondents agreed or strongly agreed that Accountable Care Organizations will be a permanent model for risk sharing with payers in years ahead.
- 63% of respondents disagreed or strongly disagreed that "the elimination of fee-for-service incentives in favor of value-based payments will hurt the quality of care provided patients."
- 58% of respondents agreed or strongly agreed that transparency about physicians' business dealings is a positive trend for the profession.

Also of interest is that a majority believe physician leaders are more likely to be able to improve physician satisfaction levels within the profession than non-physician leaders. More than half of the respondents identified physician leadership as being key to achieving success within their organizations.

Surveys and the data generated are imperfect research tools. Nonetheless, the information gleaned can provide insights on where to focus further research. Corroborating the survey data by repeating the survey in other audiences also can provide improved understanding of the issues.

A broader approach toward value also is being developed around how to redefine the value equation for healthcare. There are numerous subcomponents for quality that require better definition and clarity. Creating improved quality has proved elusive for healthcare.

Managing price (or cost) is now recognized as one of the most poorly understood aspects of the healthcare industry. Transparency, microeconomics, macroeconomics, and institutional financial or accounting strategies all contribute to this difficulty in managing the denominator of the value equation.

In the midst of this complexity, who is judging value? The patients? Physicians? Other providers? Health systems and hospitals? Obviously, redefining value will take some time and involve a variety of vested parties.

In my opinion, the physician workforce is still optimally placed to help bridge the gap toward an improved, value-driven healthcare system. It is a system that will drive value to patients and organizations, one that is highly efficient, safe, and with measurement that is able to effectively demonstrate optimal quality of care.

CHAPTER 8

Metrics, Measurement, and Patient Safety Reporting

A t its most basic, our clinical care practices have an historical basis on research and education — both of which rely on metrics, measurement, unbiased evaluation, and reporting. Unfortunately, the science for measurement of clinical care practices, and related outcomes, continues to be relatively immature. The subsequent reporting, therefore, is often inexact.

Physicians are well recognized as a professional group where data is highly valued, and the integrity of that data is considered to be pivotal for decision-making. In fact, this expectation by physicians for quality data is often recognized to filter into their decision-making for non-clinical situations as well. Subsequently, when data for any given situation becomes suspect from physicians' vantage points, the outputs generated from that data are usually suspect as well.

For clinical situations, learning how to obtain good outcomes when having to make care decisions with incomplete or flawed data becomes part of the "art" in medicine. Fortunately, the vast majority of physicians are able to refine this art successfully. Finding that balance in the non-clinical arena, however, can become even more challenging and occasionally frustrating for many physicians.

The National Quality Forum (NQF) developed and published an excellent report in February 2011 regarding consensus standards for public reporting of safety data.[1] In participating with the development of this report, I came to appreciate the importance for the following guiding principles of public reporting:

1. Entities that provide public reports of patient safety information are accountable for the quality of the reports they produce, including the timeliness and accuracy of information and the relevance and usefulness of the information to the decision-making of consumers.

2. Public reports of patient safety event information should heighten collective public awareness and concern about safety in a way that stimulates providers, healthcare organizations, and entities responsible for setting public policy to make improvements.

3. Publicly reported information about patient safety events must be previewed for accuracy by those about whom it is reported, corrected as necessary, and then displayed in ways that facilitate appropriate and informed decision-making by consumers.

4. To facilitate understanding and accountability, public reporters must use tested tools to properly convey information about the wide array of event characteristics, including those that occur frequently and those that occur rarely or with low frequency.

5. The accuracy and completeness of information in public reports should be verifiable through means such as audits, crosschecks with multiple data sources, attestations by reporting organizations, and/or other means.

6. Because the science that underpins public reporting is evolving, it is important that public reports are continually assessed for usefulness and validity and revised as the science improves.

7. To advance improvements in understanding and improving patient safety, it is essential to bring uniformity to definitions, patient safety measurement tools, and approaches to analysis and classification of events.

8. Information in public reports should be presented in a way that increases consumers' awareness and understanding of patient safety events, including preventability, by providing context, ex-

planations, and information about their role in improving patient safety for themselves and others.

9. Consumer involvement in the development of patient safety public reports is particularly important because of the significance of the information and its propensity to be highly technical in both terms and definitions.

10. Translating this information into useful, actionable tools requires the active involvement of consumers in report construction. Patient confidentiality must be maintained.

11. Complete transparency of methodology and sources should be required for all measures included in public reports.

The guiding principles listed from this NQF report work together as an interconnected set. While much of this information is focused on safety events, I believe the collective set provides important guidance for metrics, measurement, and reporting in general. I strongly encourage increased adoption of these guiding principles. In this process, physician leaders should also endeavor to become more aware of the constellation of measurement and reporting initiatives that continue to crop-up and evolve around the country, as well as in other countries. They are here to stay!

From my perspective, the good news is that this type of measurement and reporting in healthcare is evolving rapidly and that in recent years the quality of the science behind measurement has garnered increased support on many levels. All industries need metrics, measurement, and reporting in order to improve.

REFERENCE

1. National Voluntary Consensus Standards for Public Reporting of Patient Safety Event Information: A Consensus Report. National Quality Forum. Washington, DC; 2010. http://www.qualityforum.org/Publications/2011/02/National_Voluntary_Consensus_Standards_for_Public_Reporting_of_Patient_Safety_Event_Information.aspx.

CHAPTER 9

Safety, Transparency, and Physician Leadership

A ttending a high-profile conference on patient safety, I was struck by a few things. First, and most unfortunately, it was a déjà vu experience. Before becoming CEO of the AAPL, I spent many years working in patient safety, nationally and internationally. My déjà vu feeling came from recognizing that more than a decade later I was still hearing essentially the same issues being raised at the conference — the same issues that our healthcare system has not been able to solve for years.

Second, a question resurfaced for me: What other industry would consistently tolerate 30% waste and inefficiency coupled with a 10% significant error rate? Yes, U.S. healthcare is essentially a free-market economy, has numerous sectors competing for a portion of that economy, and compared to other industries is relatively unregulated by oversight agencies. Yes, the system has numerous aspects that are the envy of other countries. But as I was reminded again, we still have much to learn and gain in terms of creating large-scale change that will be sustainable over time.

These initial comments should not be construed as another gloom-and-doom piece. By nature, I am optimistic and remain strongly positive on the direction we are headed as these complex issues and problems continue to be addressed. There is much to be proud of within our healthcare system and the collective approaches toward improvement.

However, the current era of efforts toward improved patient safety and higher quality in healthcare is now more than 20 years in the making. Although there are numerous success stories within a host of clinical delivery systems, ongoing disappointment at a macro level persists, and we have not made enough significant progress as quickly as we had hoped.

Collectively, one can recognize that we continue to grapple with core systems-oriented problems that clearly affect the individuals trying to work successfully on care delivery. Progress has been slow, but at least now it is recognizable, and ongoing efforts are becoming more successful. Continuing on the positive side, several secondary aspects related to safety and quality for healthcare have gradually emerged in this evolutionary process of industry change. We can and do continue to learn from other industries while we also continue to grasp the concepts of implementing innovation better at system levels. This has been critically important for our industry to appreciate.

Nonetheless, in my opinion, how we create ongoing change for healthcare will be contingent on creating systems and processes designed by expert healthcare providers that are appropriately relevant for delivering positive change in healthcare delivery — especially for patients, families, and individual providers.

An important aspect to focus on is transparency. We all recognize how the healthcare industry primarily has revolved for decades around the knowledge and decision-making of physicians. The shift from a traditionally paternalistic approach by physicians toward truly patient-centered care with shared decision-making is certainly underway — and appropriately so.

Inevitably though, errors occur and will continue to occur during clinical care. Therefore, an important related aspect of shared decision-making also is sharing of information on processes and outcomes of care, regardless of their nature. With all physicians considered as leaders at some level, do we truly understand and fully appreciate the pivotal importance of transparency for physician leadership? Additionally, the perspective on what constitutes transparency can be highly variable. The patients' perspective? Physicians? Other providers? Health systems and hospitals? Risk managers and our legal system? The general public and lay media?

Further, the infrastructure required to support effective transparency and the complexity of processes for interdisciplinary cooperation that assures transparency across the various sectors of the industry are a heavier burden than initially appreciated.

When all is functioning smoothly and outcomes are optimal, then transparency is easy. When errors or glitches happen and less optimal outcomes are generated, then system fault lines are exposed. Communications are derailed if a transparency system and culture have not been adequately designed or implemented. Animosity, even hostility, may be a result.

Transparency is much more than sharing positive information or providing an apology with disclosure when a negative outcome occurs. Physicians play a vital role in setting expectations for themselves and the systems in which they practice. Our inputs are critical for designing, implementing and maintaining effective systems for ensuring transparency across the continuum of care, as well as across the continuum of our healthcare and legal systems. That's a tall order!

Without effective physician leadership, transparency initiatives potentially will be designed and implemented inside healthcare that are not optimally oriented to patients and their physicians, or other providers who are delivering care. With that 30% waste and 10% error rate, pressures to improve our systems are inevitable. The ongoing pressure for increased transparency similarly will be assured.

In my opinion, the physician workforce is optimally placed to drive the processes for expanding the benefits of transparency in healthcare and to help further drive a true value-based system. A system that provides value to patients and organizations is highly efficient, safe, and able to effectively demonstrate optimal quality of care in a transparent fashion.

Professionalism

CHAPTER 10

Trust: Professionalism, Altruism, Forbearance

"Philosophy does not promise to secure anything external for man, otherwise it would be admitting something that lies beyond its proper subject matter. For as the material of the carpenter is wood, and that of statuary bronze, so the subject matter of the art of living is each person's own life."

— EPICTETUS
Discourses 1.15.2

It was during a particularly difficult end-of-life family discussion a few years back that I was reacquainted with just how hostile patient families can behave in the hospital environment at times. The exact details are not important now, but the near-frenzied altercation resulted in my having to alert our more-senior hospital leadership of the situation. While heading toward the C-suite, a kindly pastor who had witnessed the events sidled up beside me for the walk down "mahogany row."

The pastor had assumed I needed consoling and was there to offer spiritual support, or so she thought. What took the pastor by surprise was my comment somewhat along the lines of, "I am always impressed by how the people who are creating the most grief for me at any point are the same people who help me to learn the most about my thoughts and attitudes." To my surprise, the pastor seemed shocked by this approach and was curious about why this was my philosophy toward difficult situations. Apparently, this particular pastor had not yet been exposed to alternatives of thought when faced with complex situations or difficult families. Consolation was a more operative approach for her.

Subsequently, once the situation settled with all parties calmed and the institution being looked upon favorably by the family, the pastor and I settled into a discourse on professionalism as the combination of all the qualities that are connected with trained and skilled people. In so doing, we both came to appreciate how different our individual philosophies were and how they had been so strongly shaped by the professional expectations set during our respective training. It also encouraged me to always respect how, as physicians, we each need to listen for the differences out there and to see what can be learned from others—professional or nonprofessional.

The words "profession" and "professional" come from the Latin word *professio*, which means a public declaration with the force of a promise. The traditional professions are medicine, law, education, and clergy. The marks of a profession are:[1]

- Competence in a specialized body of knowledge and skill;
- An acknowledgment of specific duties and responsibilities toward the individuals it serves and toward society; and
- The right to train, admit, discipline, and dismiss its members for failure to sustain competence or observe the duties and responsibilities.

Professionalism requires that practitioners strive for excellence in the following areas, which should be modeled by mentors and teachers and become part of the attitudes, behaviors, and skills integral to patient care:[1]

- **Altruism:** A physician is obligated to attend to the best interest of patients, rather than self-interest.
- **Accountability:** Physicians are accountable to their patients, to society on issues of public health, and to their profession.

- **Excellence:** Physicians are obligated to make a commitment to lifelong learning.
- **Duty:** A physician should be available and responsive when "on call," accepting a commitment to service within the profession and the community.
- **Honor and integrity:** Physicians should be committed to being fair, truthful, and straightforward in their interactions with patients and the profession.
- **Respect for others:** A physician should demonstrate respect for patients and their families, other physicians and team members, medical students, residents, and fellows.

Of these six areas, each strikes a chord that resonates deeply. But for me, it is altruism that continues to provide the most resonance for continuing on the professional route chosen. By definition, altruism is the attitude of caring about others and doing acts that help them, although one does not get anything for one's self by doing those acts. For whatever reason in my core psychology, altruism seems to help me in times of duress and certainly provides a sense of personal comfort even during times of success. I trust and depend on my altruism as a consistent compass bearing — a proverbial true north, if you will.

However, as we all recognize, in today's healthcare industry, there is clearly much to be concerned about and so many complexities to manage among a wide range of competing priorities. Idealism is easy to speak of, and yet quite difficult to enact upon on a regular basis. Our patience and commitment to the six components of professionalism are challenged on a daily basis routinely. And many of our peers are struggling with maintaining balanced views on professional and personal issues. We are indeed in a period of time when challenges may often seem to be more common than successes.

With this complexity, there is an even greater need for each of us (young or old) to look deep into what drives us as physicians. What drives us to be leaders in society? What makes us want to create larger change in the world? And what kinds of changes — or resurrection of core beliefs — are needed by each of us to make our chosen profession more satisfying? It is a profession that still carries the opportunity for us to achieve that intense professional satisfaction we all know exists.

From time to time, I will read about the ancient Stoic philosophies. Stoicism teaches the development of self-control and fortitude as a means of overcoming destructive emotions. The philosophy holds that becoming a clear and unbiased thinker allows one to understand the universal reason (logos).

One such concept within Stoicism is that of "forbearance," a term describing the quality of being patient and being able to forgive someone or to control oneself in a difficult situation. I bring this up in the context of professionalism and altruism because it can provide an increased sense of purpose when our own life's compass might be wavering. Forbearance also can be used when considering the need to be patient while waiting for difficult times to pass and the return of more positive activities and influences within one's life.

We must all live our own lives in a healthy, balanced fashion to minimize the untoward effects of this demanding profession. Giving of ourselves, while honorable and uplifting, can be draining at times. Reflecting on our core values, beliefs, and ideals will help to maintain the balance needed. Forbearance helps buffer the times when we might feel a vacillation of our core.

Please do not mistake this suggestion of forbearance as a synonym for that old catchphrase of "just suck it up, grin and bear it." We all have already had our fair share of dosing on delayed gratification. Forbearance is much deeper. It is a philosophy (among many) that can help us stay connected to ourselves and to the worlds in which we choose to live. We all have a purpose and passion to which we resonate. The suggestion is to simply have forbearance as we each continue to seek those passions and purposes we cherish.

And for a real shift in your perspective on our importance and the need for some forbearance, take a look at this YouTube video from famed astronomer Carl Sagan: "Pale Blue Dot" at https://www.youtube.com/watch?v=GO5FwsblpT8. The hope is that you become uplifted and energized at a deeper level while you further consider how to be a better leader — to yourself and all those around you.

I encourage each of us to continue seeking deeper levels for how we continue to draw upon our beliefs in the qualities of professionalism, altruism, and forbearance. We can generate positive influence in this at all levels.

REFERENCE

1. Jonsen AR, with Braddock CH III and Edwards KA. Professionalism, University of Washington's "Ethics in Medicine" program. http://depts.washington.edu/bhdept/ethics-medicine/bioethics-topics/detail/75.

CHAPTER 11

Patient-Centered Care: Is It Really Disruption?

Being somewhat of an idealist and altruistic individual, as a surgical trainee in Montreal at McGill University, I was highly influenced by a seemingly omnipresent influence of William Osler. The Osler Library is located at McGill University's Medical School, and the auditorium where our surgical educational sessions were conducted had a large portrait of Osler hanging in constant view. Like many, I endeavored to emulate his teachings and to practice by those ideologies. I just could not shake his stare from that portrait — you know, the type of portrait where the eyes are always following you.

Sir William Osler (1849-1919) was a Canadian physician who created the first residency program for specialty training of physicians, and he brought medical students out of the lecture hall for bedside clinical training. He frequently has been described as the "Father of Modern Medicine," and his career traversed the universities of McGill (1874-1884), Pennsylvania (1884-1889), Johns Hopkins (1889-1905), and Oxford (1905-1919).

A prolific writer, he once wrote in an essay titled *Books and Men* that, "He who studies medicine without books sails an uncharted sea, but he who studies medicine without patients does not go to sea at all." He also is credited for saying, "Listen to your patient; he is telling you the diagnosis," emphasizing the need to take a good history.

In a similar vein of thought, who in medicine has not heard of Florence Nightingale? Her influence on patient care has been omnipresent in our industry, primarily through her role in founding the modern nursing profession. Nightingale (1820-1910) rose to prominence managing nurses she trained during the Crimean War, where she organized the tending of wounded soldiers and gave nursing a highly favorable reputation. She became the iconic "Lady with the Lamp" while making rounds at night.

An English social reformer and statistician, Nightingale established a nursing school at London's St. Thomas' Hospital in 1860. Now part of King's College London, it was the world's first secular nursing school. Also a prolific writer, she worked to improve healthcare for all sections of British society, and advocated for hunger relief in India, to abolish prostitution laws that were overly harsh to women, and to expand female employment. In partial recognition of her pioneering work, new nurses take the Nightingale Pledge. She helped set an example of compassion and commitment to patient care, as well as diligent and thoughtful hospital administration. Indeed, patient-centered care actually has been a focus for roughly 150 years.

Patient-centered care is taking on new meaning, however, while the primary focus on physicians being the dominant conduit for care and decision-making remains. Since the mid-to-late 1800s, the complexities of healthcare delivery systems have escalated logarithmically. We all know, and feel, the diversity of influences (too many to list) that now encroach on the core components of essential patient care — the patient-physician relationship and the patient-nurse relationship in a conducive environment for optimal care.

A portion of what is gradually occurring is the rapid adoption of technologies and the progressive implementation of not only expanded responsibilities for non-physician providers but also an expanded number of non-physician clinicians involved with patient care. Several components of a new paradox gradually are becoming clearer—the paradox between existing delivery systems oriented toward how altruistic physicians prefer to deliver care versus a renewed focus on patient-centered care that is trying to thrive in a highly complex set of evolving systems amid new types of providers not yet fully oriented to patients.

Disruption of our industry is at the core of this paradox. Learning to manage it effectively will be a challenge for physician leadership and everyone oriented toward truly successful patient-centered care.

Communication, communication, communication . . . we all know it is an essential component of healthcare. When things go incredibly well, communication, caring, and compassion are most often at the core of success. Equally, however, when things go horribly wrong in healthcare, communication problems are usually at the core.

Among many examples, electronic health records gradually have gained acceptance in healthcare. Cloud-based data warehousing and assertive efforts with data analytics are common practices. Push messaging that results from the analytics is now prevalent. Social media channels are generally accepted, and expected, forms of communication. But what is less clear is the collective and eventual impact on healthcare delivery, especially when patient expectations are higher than provider willingness.

Our personal lives have been pervasively affected — and relatively quickly — by technology as all generations are now seemingly dependent on digital devices for information, and a new form of addictive dependency apparently is evolving. Interpersonal communication and the types of relationships being formed are in unprecedented transition. A new type of patient-physician relationship is developing gradually, but is not yet formalized.

The Internet is propelling clinicians into new ethical and legal territory, raising questions about the accuracy of online information, patients' right to privacy, and doctors' liability regarding their patients' online behavior.

Liliya Gershengoren, a psychiatrist and professor with Weill Cornell Medicine, concluded from a survey she conducted that an overwhelming majority of psychiatrists and residents at one U.S. academic hospital had Googled a patient at some point in their careers. These survey results were presented at an annual meeting of the American Psychiatric Association.[1] Of 48 staff doctors and 34 residents who responded anonymously, 93% of staff and 94% of residents reported researching a patient online at least once. She found that 17% of staff and 40% of residents Googled their patients on a frequent or semi-regular basis in the emergency department (compared to 5% of staff and 15% of residents in inpatient settings).

And then there are external risks — malevolent forces that continually try to create chaos by penetrating our organizational technology with the intention of stealing patient data, holding patient care networks for ransom, or even doing harm to patients.

As physicians, we must continually seek how to optimize patient-centered care in the face of ever-increasing change and complexity. We must also continue to seek how our role as the natural, intended leaders in the healthcare system (and the dominant focus of patient care) can be further optimized. Increased personal awareness in both these areas will be essential for achieving improved outcomes on both fronts. Managing any paradox is not about "yes" or "no" decisions — it is a process of finding, then managing, the balance for both the individuals and organizations we influence. Positive outcomes often result from disruption.

I encourage all of us to continue seeking deeper levels of understanding. Proactively helping others, as physician leaders, to better manage the disruptive paradox of true patient-centered care is a critical component of our professional responsibility.

REFERENCE

1. https://www.psychcongress.com/article/most-psychiatric-professionals-google-their-patients-survey-finds

CHAPTER 12

Caring and Compassion vs. Physician Compensation

Years ago, I was approached by someone in distress over a newly made, poor-prognosis medical diagnosis. Yes, this happens to each of us routinely. But what made me stop to reflect after my discussion was the reflex reaction I had to feel empathy and to show genuine concern for the person without considering any other issues before engaging with her. It was an inherent response that, I believe, always lies just under the emotional surface for each of us as physicians.

Caring for people is a privilege and an honor we should continually cherish. There are very few professions, or even other work environments, where people show up and expect to share their deepest anxieties, troubles, and secrets. Physicians are trained to receive this information in trusted confidence, and our patients usually want to use us this way. It is often a part of their healing — knowing that a caring person listened and demonstrated genuine concern.

In our perpetual quest to ferret out details on potential disease states in our patients, and to manage the excessive amount of related information, we should never forget this basic premise: We are basically here to care for people, and it is an instinctual drive for us as individuals that carries tremendous potential satisfaction in doing so effectively. Satisfaction for our patients . . . and ourselves.

At about the same time I was approached by the person mentioned, I also had the opportunity to attend a conference related to the well-being of physicians. It was co-sponsored by the American Medical Association, British Medical Association, and Canadian Medical Association, a relatively new annual meeting called the International Conference on Physician Health. That year's theme: increasing joy in medicine.

We are all aware of the concern on morale within the physician workforce (including trainees). It is likely there was some implicit bias among the attendees, but an overwhelming undertone I consistently detected throughout the conference was the compassion physicians continue to have for their patients, knowing the critically important role physicians have in patients' lives. At every session and in each discussion forum, there always was a comment of some type related to compassion.

It was easy to recognize the high levels of compassion for patients and the desire to remain as compassionate caregivers. This recognition was important for all attendees but also important for me personally. I have been away from direct patient care many years now but remain highly engaged with safety and quality initiatives. Appreciating once again the drive that most physicians carry toward being compassionate caregivers further affirms my drive for the important work of helping all physicians become better leaders.

So how do we ensure we do not lose our core value of compassion, and actually better leverage it?

An important concept still being delineated in a variety of social sciences is that of self-compassion. To some degree, it is that old mantra of looking after yourself so you can look after others better. And yet it is more than simply eating well, getting plenty of exercise, and obtaining good sleep. There is an emerging recognition that treating ourselves kindly and compassionately (emotionally and psychologically), as we would treat a patient, can be vitally important to our general well-being and sense of happiness. This translates to a more-positive approach to our daily lives and to improved interactions with others — especially patients and our families.

Enter alternative payment models. How will this evolving payment system create compassion and improve our caring for people?

There is no simple answer to that question. There is, however, an important recognition for us all — value-based payment methodologies are here for the foreseeable future. Unfortunately, there are several tests and experimental models that will be present for the next few years. We cannot predict the future, but we can know the direction it is headed.

In November 2016, the Department of Health and Human Services (HHS) finalized its policy implementing the Merit-Based Incentive Payment System and the Advanced Alternative Payment Models incentive payment provisions in the Medicare Access and CHIP Reauthorization Act of 2015 (aka MACRA). Collectively, it is called the Quality Payment Program.

According to HHS, the Quality Payment Program gradually will transform Medicare payments for more than 600,000 clinicians across the country. HHS considers it a major step in improving care across the entire healthcare system. The Quality Payment Program, which replaces the flawed Sustainable Growth Rate, is designed to give clinicians the tools and flexibility to provide high-quality, patient-centered care.

Further, this initiative offers a fresh start for Medicare by focusing payments around the care that is best for the patients, providing more options to clinicians for innovative care and payment approaches, and reducing administrative burden to give clinicians more time to spend with their patients, instead of on paperwork. With clinicians as partners, HHS built a system that delivers better care — one in which clinicians work together and fully understand patients' needs, Medicare pays for what works and spends taxpayer money more wisely, and patients are in the center of their care. The result: a healthier country.

So where does compensation fit in? There are a variety of groups delivering benchmark surveys of physician compensation. These are important sources of information, and physicians should review them on an annual or bi-annual basis. It is important to know the market value of your discipline, because it helps you negotiate fair compensation arrangements.

Being psychologically assured your compensation is at, or near, market value certainly contributes to a better sense of self-worth and personal happiness. If you are not near market value, then it is also good to know that information for negotiation purposes.

Balancing core values with fair financial reward is a complex affair, especially when the external influences on both seem to be beyond our personal control and our ability to influence outcomes directly.

Learning to look after ourselves with a certain degree of self-compassion will help — mainly by contributing to a calmer and happier disposition. Focusing on our patients by drawing on our core values, such as caring for people and our inherent compassion, also will contribute to a better balance. Keeping up with evolving trends and learning how to anticipate them, even though you cannot control them, helps you manage change. And knowing your value in the marketplace helps you ensure appropriate reward for the compassionate quality care you and your team provide patients.

By the way, the person who approached me with a poor prognosis had followed an expected clinical course and did not live past the calendar year. Before she passed, she wrote me a thank-you note that brought tears to my eyes. In it, she mentioned how often she reflected on the kind, caring words of advice I provided in her moment of need. Apparently, my words continued to give her strength and courage as she received treatment for a hopeless situation. Her words to me are more than enough compensation.

Regardless of your career stage or chronological age, it is important to reflect routinely on your core values — caring for people and compassion being only two. In this reflection, there also is opportunity to reframe the value that you contribute to your environment. What is your value-based contribution to your patients and to yourself? It is not just about the money, but you should be at fair-market value.

CHAPTER 13

Obliging Differences During Times of Pestilence

The term *noblesse oblige* refers to the unwritten obligation of privileged people to act with generosity and nobility toward those less privileged. Many people view the medical profession, and by extension those practicing medicine, as privileged. When society is under less pressure and the economy more robust, the profession comes under scrutiny and criticism by many who might contend that physicians do not do enough to fulfill their commitment toward *noblesse oblige*.

A few things during the COVID-19 pandemic, however, turned the calloused view of our profession to a more positive one. Appreciation for the healthcare workforce and related allied professionals was high, with an ongoing outpouring of support and public gratitude. People better recognized the essential service medical professionals provide and acknowledged their dedicated commitment to caring for others during times of crisis. The general population came to understand that without this essential component of society's infrastructure — a committed healthcare workforce, and specifically with physicians leading care teams — the population would be far worse off. The public views physicians as confident, and their trust in physicians has escalated.

What is more, the general public better understands that healthcare workers place themselves in harm's way by working on the frontlines of care during a pandemic. Many other workers are also on the frontlines and are at increased risk (*e.g.*, grocery store workers), but none are at greater risk than healthcare workers.

Unfortunately, many healthcare workers fell ill during the pandemic and an untold number died. We still do not have a firm understanding of the magnitude of the negative mental health effects, such as burnout or PTSD. How many of our fellow physicians and our non-physician co-workers had to change their lives as a result? We likely will never know the true number.

During times such as these, it is not uncommon to reflect on history and philosophy to gain further insights. *The Plague,* a novel written by philosopher/writer Albert Camus in 1947, is a story focusing on a physician and the people he works with and treats in an Algerian port town that is struck by the bubonic plague.[1] This particular work deals with issues central to three different but related philosophies: existentialism, the absurd, and humanism.

Existentialism is a philosophical approach that usually emphasizes the existence of the individual person as a free and responsible agent determining their own development through acts of free will. The townsfolk in Camus's novel "were not more to blame than others; they forgot to be modest, that was all, and thought that everything still was possible for them; which presupposed that pestilences were impossible. They went on doing business, arranged for journeys, and formed views. How should they have given a thought to anything like plague, which rules out any future, cancels journeys, silences the exchange of views. They fancied themselves free, and no one will ever be free so long as there are pestilences" (1.5.3). Similarly, one can argue that during much of 2020, many citizens "fancied themselves free" amid the active pandemic; parallel actions were noted in previous influenza epidemics.

Where the balance sits between free will and respect for others in a successful democracy, however, is often a point of significant debate. Being a "responsible agent" for an existential approach, as noted above, is often lost on a few members of our society. Specific to the recent pandemic, healthcare workers were caught in the crossfire of preferences — at times, to their own health's detriment.

Unfortunately, despite knowledge of the ramifications, many in healthcare pursued their own detrimental behavior. When I asked some about their behaviors, they often recognized the absurdity of their actions, but proceeded nonetheless. "Throughout the day the doctor was conscious that the slightly dazed feeling that came over him whenever he thought about the plague was growing more pronounced. Finally he realized that he was afraid! On two occasions he entered crowded cafes . . . he felt a need for friendly contacts, human warmth. A stupid instinct, Rieux told himself; still, it served to remind him that he'd promised to visit the traveling salesman" (Camus 1.8.46).

The need for human warmth and a sense of community can be potentially dangerous during a pandemic, but fear is part of the terror of plague-like conditions. To combat mental anguish, it seems, many people are willing to subject themselves to the possibility of physical anguish, possibly death. There were numerous examples from large-scale gatherings where appropriate safety precautions were ignored and outbreaks inevitably occurred. Many would argue this is an example of *absurdity*.

Part of what makes any epidemic or pandemic so difficult for people is that often they do not know or understand why they are being forced to suffer; there is no rational explanation. For Camus' townsfolk, "Father Paneloux's sermon simply brought home the fact that they had been sentenced, for an unknown crime, to an indeterminate period of punishment" (2.4.1). For many, this suffering is viewed as senseless, and it creates deep levels of anxiety and, to some degree, abnormal behaviors compared to their normal routines.

Returning to the subject of physicians and healthcare workers, from my perspective, professionalism is based on the core philosophy of *humanism*. Humanist beliefs typically stress the potential value and goodness of human beings, emphasize common human needs, and seek solely rational ways of solving human problems. "If, as was most likely, it died out, all would be well. If not, one would know . . . what steps should be taken for coping with and finally overcoming it. The doctor opened his window . . . . There lay certitude; there, in the daily round. . . . The thing was to do your job as it should be done" (Camus 1.5.8-9).

Professionalism is an indispensable element in the compact between the medical profession and society that is based on trust and putting the needs of patients above all other considerations.[2] The topic of professionalism is receiving renewed attention as a result of the pandemic, but also because we are in a time of change regarding how to engender a sense of professionalism during all stages of a medical career. A core component of professionalism is obliging differences while caring for others. In so doing, each of us is responsible for continuing to approach the impact of the pandemic from a humanistic vantage and to draw deeply from our core altruism and belief in people's inherent goodness as humans.

"They knew now that if there is one thing one can always yearn for and sometimes attain, it is human love" (Camus 5.4.14). As we all knew, the pandemic would eventually pass, and the resilience of the human spirit prevails as our entire world accommodates the changes the pandemic imposed. An essential piece of the human spirit is that innate desire and ability to provide and receive human love — and to provide love to others less fortunate than we. Being a physician is indeed a wonderful privilege that should be honored and cherished; therefore, I encourage all of us to seek and re-define our own sense of *noblesse oblige* as we continue to move forward, while also continuing to oblige the differences imposed on us as a result of the pandemic.

REFERENCES

1. Camus A. *La Peste* (French). Paris: Gallimard; 1947.

2. Brennan MD, Monson, V. Professionalism: Good for Patients and Health Care Organizations. *Mayo Clinic Proceedings*. 2014;89(5):644–52, https:// www.mayoclinic proceedings.org/article/S0025-6196(14)00064-0/fulltext.

CHAPTER 14

Physicians Meeting the Challenge of Contrasting Ideologies

O ur nation's healthcare industry is more complex than all other industries and will continue to be complex and create significant uncertainty. Such complexity, interestingly, seems to occur regardless of political leanings or opinions, but this uncertainty means that large numbers of patients and their families are being negatively affected.

Remember: The number one reason why people file for bankruptcy continues to be related to healthcare debt.[1]

Growing up in Midwest North America, I distinctly remember a multitude of societal opinions that often carried distinct bias and deeply engrained ideology. Of course, while I was young, I did not understand these words, let alone the nature of the behaviors they represented. Going through medical school, I gradually became aware of these human attributes and how they impacted not only clinical care but also management decisions that eventually influenced educational approaches. For example, our medical school class was subjected to a unilateral decision that we all had to receive BCG vaccination against tuberculosis. At the time, it was a relatively untested approach of unproven value — and no member of the class was given the option of not receiving the vaccination. Given the nature of our training environment at the time, and the social diversity of patients passing through the system, I still argue that this was not a public health-oriented decision, but one of implicit bias and regional ideology within the leadership of the school.

Behaviors, or actions, are predicated on individual and collective values, beliefs, and ideals. Behaviors influence our cultures and ultimately the environments within which we live, work, and play. Leadership, and the behavior of leaders, is what influences a culture most significantly. Creating a healthy culture is pivotal for improving the healthcare industry, and healthcare leadership must take special care to manage implicit biases and contrasting ideologies through exceptional behavior.

Perhaps it is a bit remedial, but covering a few basic definitions can be a helpful reminder about what drives our behaviors and actions.

- **Values:** Important and lasting beliefs or ideals shared by the members of a culture about what is good or bad and desirable or undesirable. (Source: *Business Dictionary*)
- **Beliefs:** Assumptions and convictions that are held to be true by an individual or a group, regarding concepts, events, people and things. (Source: *Business Dictionary*)
- **Ideals:** Persons or things conceived as embodying such a conception, and conforming to such a standard, they are taken as a model for imitation. (Source: Dictionary.com)
- **Ideology:** A system of ideas that explains and lends legitimacy to actions and beliefs of a social, religious, political, or corporate entity. (Source: *Business Dictionary*)
- **Implicit bias:** Refers to the attitudes or stereotypes that affect our understanding, actions, and decisions in an unconscious manner. These biases, which encompass both favorable and unfavorable assessments, are activated involuntarily and without an individual's awareness or intentional control. (Source: Kirwan Institute for the Study of Race and Ethnicity, Ohio State University.)
- **Consensus:** The middle ground in decision-making, between total assent and total disagreement. It depends upon participants having

shared values and goals, and on having broad agreement on specific issues and overall direction. It implies everyone accepts and supports the decision, and understands the reasons for making it. (Source: *Business Dictionary*)

Patient care is all about people. Clinical delivery systems are all about teams of people working well together. And the patient-physician relationship remains one of the most intimate, trusted, and caring of human relationships known.

All physicians are leaders at some level, and leadership is ultimately about people — regardless of clinical discipline or nonclinical activity. The leadership that physicians provide, whether informally or formally, is still a dominant influence for the culture of healthcare.

The values, beliefs, and ideals of physician behavior remain central to one of our profession's sacred guides, the Hippocratic Oath; it is perhaps the most widely known of Greek medical texts. The oath requires physicians to promise to uphold a number of professional ethical standards. Here are a few excerpts:

"In purity and according to divine law will I carry out my life and my art."

"Into whatever homes I go, I will enter them for the benefit of the sick, avoiding any voluntary act of impropriety or corruption, including the seduction of women or men, whether they are free men or slaves."

"Whatever I see or hear in the lives of my patients, whether in connection with my professional practice or not, which ought not to be spoken of outside, I will keep secret, as considering all such things to be private."

"So long as I maintain this oath faithfully and without corruption, may it be granted to me to partake of life fully and the practice of my art, gaining the respect of all men for all time."

Let us all reinvigorate in consideration of that oath as we seek ways to augment the professionalism that has carried the health and culture of the industry for so many generations. Incoming physicians, and those established in careers, readily gravitate to the altruistic side of the spectrum for these values, beliefs, and ideals. It is our collective altruism that shapes our individual as well as collective behaviors. Altruism can be considered a core ideology for physicians.

The past few decades have challenged physicians' roles in healthcare and in society as a whole. The recent shift to a value-based model of care delivery is likely to survive and become the predominant focus for care delivery. Compared to the recent past, physicians now have a fresh opportunity to demonstrate leadership at all levels. The opportunity for influence by physicians will help shape the evolving culture of healthcare in coming years. Physicians value "value."

The inherent complexity of healthcare creates the perpetual expectation for change. We must all be comfortable with this reality. Even with the variety of value-based approaches on our horizon, significant swings in our industry already are occurring. As another important figure from ancient Greek history, the philosopher Heraclitus, once said, "The only constant is change." That readily applies to healthcare.

The vagaries of national politics contribute to constant change, regardless of which party is in control. Obviously, physicians will have opinions and debates not only on politics in general, but also on the impact of politics on healthcare specifically. In these discussions, contrasting ideologies certainly will surface and, at times, create consternation.

As leaders, physicians also have the opportunity to use their influence to facilitate healthy, balanced discussions while also helping their local, regional, or national environments achieve stability in the face of contrasting ideologies. Again, physicians are leaders, and leaders create culture through their influence — not only in their decisions but also through their individual, daily behaviors. Physician-oriented values, beliefs, and ideals can provide the voice of reason when contrasting ideologies are present. Where change is constant, leadership also should be constant — to provide the optimal pathway through shifting circumstances. Physicians are positioned to provide balance and direction within healthcare during periods of intense change. Let us all rise to the occasion and not become excessively distracted by contrasting ideologies.

While pursuing my academic career in trauma surgery, followed now by more than a decade of leadership roles nationally and internationally, I have come to realize that contrasting ideologies are always active on a routine basis. The implicit biases that are related to them create the diversity of opinion that ultimately makes our world so special. Navigating ideology and implicit bias are a portion of my daily routine. In so doing, I must always be introspective and on an internal lookout for how my own implicit bias may (or may not) create decisions that are not fully optimal.

To help offset my propensity of implicit bias and ideology, I routinely seek a variety of opinions from a variety of sources that I know will not be similar to mine. I believe this is what successful leaders should do in order to make their best decisions, regardless of leadership style. Building consensus becomes simpler and decision-making more robust.

Coming from a background in surgery, it is an interesting process to continually unlearn my inherently developed surgical personality traits. Helping to proactively manage transitions in our industry is, and always has been, a critical component of our professional responsibility.

REFERENCE

1. https://ajph.aphapublications.org/doi/abs/10.2105/AJPH.2018.304901?journalCode=ajph

Communication and Relationship Management

CHAPTER 15

Self-Fulfilling Prophecies — There is More to Them Than We Think

"It is our attitude at the beginning of a difficult task which more than anything will affect a successful outcome."

— WILLIAM JAMES

"Whether you think you can, or you think you can't, you're right."

— HENRY FORD

"If you expect the battle to be insurmountable, you've met the enemy. It's you."

— KHANG KIJARRO NGUYEN

While a poor starving medical student, I once enrolled in a drug trial to get some extra cash to help pay the bills. It was only going to be a three-week trial, so what the heck — easy money, right?

The study design was set up so that each week was different but randomized in the sequence of receiving the study drug and at varying dosage levels. I got through all three weeks, but one was exceptionally horrible — the first week — fraught with headaches, nausea, general malaise, fatigue, and more. I figured I must have received the maximal dose up front and had simply adjusted to the drug's effects for the remaining two weeks. To my surprise and dismay, in the first week, the drug was a placebo! Whew, was I embarrassed!

A self-fulfilling prophecy is a psychosociological phenomenon whereby one expects something and eventually experiences the realization of this expectation simply because one anticipates it, and one's consequent conduct aligns to fulfill the original expectation.[1] As it turns out, a commonly cited example of a self-fulfilling prophecy is the placebo effect, when a person experiences certain outcomes because they expect an inactive "look-alike" substance or treatment to work, even though it has no known medical effect.

Robert Merton first introduced the term *self-fulfilling prophecy* in 1948 to denote a "false definition of the situation evoking a behavior which makes the originally false conception come true."[2] There are two types of self-fulfilling prophecies: self-imposed prophecies occur when your own expectations influence your behavior; other-imposed prophecies occur when others' expectations influence your behavior. All opinions you value can cause this prophecy.

The Pygmalion effect is a type of other-imposed self-fulfilling prophecy that states that the way you treat someone has a direct impact on how that person acts. If another person thinks something will happen, they may consciously or unconsciously make it happen through their actions or inaction. Simply put, a false reality could actually become truth due to human psychological responses to predictions, fears, and worries associated with the future.[3]

Self-fulfilling prophecy, also known as interpersonal expectancy effect, has a history and diversity of inquiry that has shown that the expectations of psychological researchers, classroom teachers, courtroom judges, business executives, and healthcare providers can unintentionally affect the responses of their research participants, pupils, jurors, employees, and patients, respectively.[4]

Self-fulfilling prophecies can yield both negative and positive results, and the interpersonal communication whereby this process often transpires can, therefore, have potentially strong implications for patient practices, physician leadership influences, and, ultimately, the healthcare industry overall.

For example, a self-fulfilling prophecy becomes a potential asset when people are labeled as having talents, strengths, abilities, and positive resources. In a seminal study, teachers were told at the beginning of a school year that certain of their students were potential late bloomers who would be expected to excel during the school year under proper guidance. Even though there was nothing that set those students apart from their peers, several months later, their schoolwork had improved considerably.

Similarly, therapists may inadvertently change the way they approach a client based on the *DSM* diagnostic label applied, such that a therapist may change the way the client is treated based on whether a negative or a positive *DSM* label is present. Just as patients who are labeled with disorders may come to internalize their negative labels, patients may come to internalize positive labels.[5,6]

In the workplace, the Pygmalion effect can have a powerful influence on job performance and career development. If supervisors are told that newly graduated trainees are "among the best" at the time they join their team, the supervisors will tend to believe the workers perform better on the job than those for whom no special designation was given. Likewise, negative connotations about a class of workers are likely to affect the way in which those employees are regarded by their supervisors. They may be appraised as not performing to standards if that is the expectation.

The Pygmalion effect is logical, once understood, and concludes that expectations alone can raise performance above — or plunge it below — established performance levels.[7] For now, just think back to how you were treated as a trainee, or recently, how you have been treating trainees or co-workers. Is it positive or negative?

Cognition, interpretation, biases, and mental processing each, among others, have a strong influence, negative or positive, on the physical and emotional reactions we all have toward stress or uncertainty. But these also represent ways by which we, as physicians, can help create a shift in the stress response toward a more positive outcome, thereby setting up the potential for positive self-fulfilling prophesies in both our professional and personal lives. Our patients, peers, and families will thank us.

Consider another example. Whenever patients enter our practice or institution during a period of crisis, their defenses are down and emotional distress is high. Beyond their illness or injury, the patient also inherently feels an urgency to decrease their level of emotional distress. Because they are motivated toward alleviating emotional distress, they are open to being influenced by the care delivery team and possibly altering their ways of thinking and behaving in a crisis.

As physicians, we can set the tone and approach not only for the patient in distress, but for the entire team of individuals involved in that immediate situation. And this approach can then be carried over into their ongoing care experience as the crisis passes. Positive emotional stability, humility, sympathy, and empathy, coupled with an obvious caring approach toward others while demonstrating supportive leadership, go a long way in creating the optimal environments of care for others. In this regard, all physicians are leaders!

When we think of our own behaviors and how to gradually shift our approaches in complex working conditions, it is important to recognize that change is stressful, even when it is beneficial. Change requires effort and conscious awareness. Five critical aspects of mental processing that play a role in stress management include:[8]

1. *Self-fulfilling prophecy.* What a person believes will happen or expects to happen sometimes influences their behavior in a way that increases the likelihood of the expected outcome. Negative expectations increase anxiety and stress. Identifying goals for

change and facing such challenges with optimism and a positive attitude will facilitate optimal coping and management.

2. *Mental imagery.* Coinciding with expectations for a given situation, a person will develop an associated mental picture and internal dialogue. This mental imagery increases anxiety and stress reactions. Positive expectations, in contrast, minimize the effects of life stressors and increase effective coping.

3. *Self-talk.* Internal dialogue takes place 24/7. Self-talk is the conversations or messages that people have with themselves. A person typically is not aware of this internal dialogue or its effect on anxiety, stress, and self-esteem. Self-talk also influences mental imagery. Negative mental images and negative self-talk can result in anxiety and psychosomatic symptoms, whereas positive self-talk encourages self-confidence, effective coping, and a general feeling of well-being.

4. *Controlling and perfectionistic behavior.* Perfectionism and unrealistic expectations often go hand in hand. Responses demonstrated by controlling and perfectionistic behaviors are frequently an effort to avoid abuse, conflict, the unknown, anxiety, or feelings of inadequacy. Placing unrealistic expectations on others is a form of controlling behavior. Self-management consumes enough energy without expanding into the realm of controlling others. Additional responses to controlling behaviors are stress, anxiety, frustration, and anger.

5. *Anger.* Anger is a normal, healthy emotion when expressed appropriately. It can be damaging to self and others when expressed inappropriately because of the internal tension or build-up that predisposes alienation and explosiveness with others. This behavior results in low self-esteem and poor interpersonal relationships. Chronic anger and hostility are related to the development or exacerbation of several physical symptoms, illnesses, and diseases.

Interestingly, confirmatory and implicit bias can be viewed as being similar to self-fulfilling prophecy. We all seek evidence that validates our prior beliefs or values and may underestimate or ignore evidence that contradicts our expectations.[9] And in a related manner, conceptual and empirical work on self-fulfilling prophecies and stigmas suggests that the anticipation of stigmatization will affect the individual's affective, cognitive, and behavioral reactions. The belief that others consider one to be inferior will usually be distressing. It can stimulate either assumption-confirming or assumption-disconfirming behavior, depending on the situation and the individual.[10]

Parenthetically, an interesting twist on a related area of creating influence through others is that the positive skew distributions of expertise, creativity, and other learned accomplishments often result from what Merton dubbed in 1968 the Matthew Effect of the rich getting richer (so named in reference to a passage in the Gospel of Matthew). Merton described the stages in which distinguished scientific careers arise: initial talent advantages, study at distinguished universities, close work with eminent professors, early and frequent publication, job placement at famous laboratories, and citation and other recognition. These events and conditions multiply one another's effects to produce highly skewed scientific creativity. As few as a tenth of the scientists may account for nearly all the significant scientific work in a given field. Though a few mavericks are exceptions, Nobel laureates and similarly distinguished scientists usually follow the Matthew pattern, which resembles wealth creation in that small initial advantages multiply over decades.[11]

The medical profession is commonly viewed as a leadership profession, both within and without the healthcare industry. Therefore, as physicians, by expressing positive expectations for ourselves, our colleagues, our organizations, our patients, our communities, and healthcare as a whole, we can contribute, individually and collectively, to creating the positive transformations needed in our industry. We have the potential to make it a self-fulfilling prophecy!

REFERENCES

1. Biggs M. Self-fulfilling Prophecies. In *The Oxford Handbook of Analytical Sociology*, eds. P Bearman and P Hedstrom, 294–314. Oxford, UK: Oxford University Press; 2011.

2. Merton RK. The Self-fulfilling Prophecy. *The Antioch Review. 1948;8(2):193–210.*

3. Schaedig D. Self-fulfilling Prophecy and the Pygmalion Effect. *Simply Psychology.* August 24, 2020. www.simplypsychology.org/self-fulfilling-prophecy.html

4. Rosenthal R. Self-Fulfilling Prophecy. In *Encyclopedia of Human Behavior (Second Edition)*, ed. VS Ramachandran, 328–335. Cambridge, MA: Academic Press;2012. www.sciencedirect.com/science/article/pii /B9780123750006003141

5. Magyar-Moe J. *Therapist's Guide to Positive Psychological Interventions.* Cambridge, MA: Academic Press;2009.

6. Macrae CN, Quadflieg S. Impression Formation. In *Encyclopedia of Human Behavior (Second Edition)*, ed. VS Ramachandran, 410–417. Cambridge, MA: Academic Press;2012.

7. McCrie R. *Security Operations Management (Third Edition).* Oxford, UK: Butterworth-Heinemann;2016.

8. Johnson SL. *Therapist's Guide to Posttraumatic Stress Disorder Intervention.* Cambridge, MA: Academic Press;2009.

9. Coulacoglou C, Saklofske DH. *Psychometrics and Psychological Assessment.* Cambridge, MA: Academic Press;2017.

10. Kravitz DA. Affirmative Action. In *Encyclopedia of Applied Psychology*, ed. CD Spielberger, 65–77. Cambridge, MA: Academic Press;2004.

11. Walberg HJ, Arian G. Distribution of Creativity. *Encyclopedia of Creativity* (Second Edition), eds. MA Runco, Pritzker SR, 397–399. Cambridge, MA: Academic Press;2011.

CHAPTER 16

Clarion Call: Elective, Urgent, or Emergent?

Without barraging us all with an excess of dismal statistics, I will simply state that worrisome data on physician workforce morale has accrued rapidly the past few years. For example, in the Medscape National Physician Burnout & Suicide Report 2020: The Generational Divide, more than 15,000 physicians surveyed identified four concerns as the leading causes of burnout: too many bureaucratic tasks, spending too many hours at work, feeling like just a cog in a wheel, and the increased computerization of practice.[1] Physicians from 29 specialties graded the severity of their burnout. The Medscape survey results rank burnout by specialty based on feedback from 15,000 physicians:

1. Urology >54%
2. Neurology >50%
3. Nephrology >49%
4. Diabetes/Endocrinology >46%
5. Radiology >46%
6. Family medicine >46%
7. Obstetrics/Gynecology >46%
8. Rheumatology >46%
9. Infectious disease >45%
10. Internal medicine >44%
11. Critical care >44%
12. Cardiology >44%
13. Emergency medicine >43%

14. Physical Medicine/Rehabilitation >43%
15. Oncology >42%
16. Pediatrics >41%
17. Anesthesiology >41%
18. Pulmonary medicine >41%
19. Allergy and Immunology >38%
20. Plastic Surgery >37%
21. Gastroenterology >36%
22. Pathology >36%
23. Dermatology >36%
24. Otolaryngology >35%
25. General surgery >35%
26. Psychiatry/Mental Health >35%
27. Orthopedics >34%
28. Ophthalmology >30%
29. Public Health and Preventive Medicine >29%

Numerous influence groups within healthcare have recognized similar trends and are calling for action. Several professional discipline organizations also have begun rolling out a host of offerings related to symptom relief, such as providing insights oriented to resilience training or how to develop a mindfulness practice. The clarion call is loud, and its focus is progressively sharpening.

Regardless of your own personal sense of discomfort, the data clearly shows that all levels of the physician workforce are being affected to some degree and with high incidence rates — from students to the most-seasoned practitioners.[2] Even if we do not personally feel it, we certainly all know someone who is feeling the burden of our industry's current complexity and is not necessarily able to live a happy, positive life.

These sets of issues fill the spectrum: from "not a problem, thanks," to "maybe I will check into it further someday," (elective) to "I recognize how it is effecting my performance," (urgent) to "I damn well better get something sorted out quick or it will all unravel on me further" (emergent). And we are all affected.

Interestingly, "burnout" is not recognized as a distinct disorder in the *Diagnostic and Statistical Manual of Mental Disorders, 5th edition.* However, it is included in the *International Classification of Diseases, Tenth Revision* (ICD-10) — not as a disorder, but under problems related to life-management difficulty. As I try to better understand the issues, it seems the view of burnout as a form of depression is finding common support.[3]

To be sure, physicians are not the only individuals struggling with predilections for burnout or less-than-optimal job satisfaction. We all know that nursing is aware of this problem, as are several other clinical and ancillary healthcare professions. As well, outside our industry, there are numerous other professions or job types (e.g., dentistry, law enforcement, factory workers, etc.) with similar issues.

While individuals might find ways to cope with symptoms of burnout (e.g., resilience training and mindfulness), to truly prevent burnout there needs to be a combination of organizational (systems) change and awareness building (education) for individuals.

Maslach and Leiter postulated that burnout occurs when there is a disconnect between the organization and the individual regarding what they called the six areas of work-life: workload, control, reward, community, fairness, and values.[4] Resolving these discrepancies requires integrated action on the part of both the individual and the organization. A better connection on workload means assuring adequate resources to meet demands as well as work-life balances that encourage employees to revitalize their energy. A better connection on values means clear organizational values to which employees can feel committed. A better connection on community means supportive leadership and relationships with colleagues rather than discord.

But let us be clear: Not everyone is burned out, nor even on the cusp of being dissatisfied with their profession. Most physicians remain happy with their choice of becoming a physician, and many continue to practice in environments that provide them deep levels of professional satisfaction. Let us not forget about these fine individuals who continue to excel while others struggle. We all have things to learn from these peers that can become transferrable skills and learned approaches on a broader level.

Those who listen to National Public Radio often enjoy Friday mornings because that is when the StoryCorps features air. StoryCorps is an independent, nonprofit project that celebrates the lives of everyday Americans by sharing their stories. A recent piece caught my attention during a commute as I was thinking about the sets of issues hitting the morale of our workforce.[5]

For 25 years, the Rev. Noel Hickie, 74, and Marcia Hilton, 70, helped families during their most trying moments. Hickie was working as a hospital chaplain and Hilton as a bereavement counselor when the two met at a hospital in Eugene, Oregon. As I listened to the segment about their work (available at storycorps.org), tears welled up and I needed to pull over from my drive for a few moments.

During my clinically active years with trauma surgery and surgical critical care, I participated in far too many end-of-life decisions and a host of individual discussions projecting the lifestyle effects of newly acquired complex disabilities. Hickie and Hilton describe caring similarly for others and how their own lives were affected, and how they both carried on in this vein for so many years because of their deep belief in the importance of helping others in difficult life situations — not for themselves as providers, but for the people affected.

I resonated with the scenarios they described, and also immediately felt a sense of deep pride in knowing that many incredibly strong individuals in our various fields continue to create highly significant impacts on others' lives through this kind of work, and how so many are able to do so because of their intense commitments and beliefs in helping others. Fortunately for us all, numerous physicians — and non-physicians such as Hickie and Hilton — are able to find or keep their balance with the six key areas of workload, control, reward, community, fairness, and values.

As physicians, we must continually seek out the uncertainty in our own lives and optimize our personal situations. Personal insight and increased awareness are essential steps for achieving improved leadership — not only for the individuals and organizations we influence, but additionally for ourselves as humans.

REFERENCES

1. Medscape National Physician Burnout & Suicide Report 2020: The Generational Divide, https://www.medscape.com/slideshow/2020-lifestyle-burnout-6012460?src=WNL_physrep_200115_burnout2020&uac=287507PN&impID=2245458&faf=1#1

2. Shanafelt TD, West CP, Sinsky C, et al. Changes in burnout and satisfaction with work-life integration in physicians and the general US working population between 2011 and 2017. *Mayo Clinic Proceedings.* 2019;94:1681-1604. https://www.mayoclinicproceedings.org/article/S0025-6196(18)30938-8/fulltext.

3. https://www.cdc.gov/nchs/icd/data/10cmguidelines-FY2019-final.pdf

4. Maslach C, Schaufeli WB, Leiter MP. Job burnout. *Annual Review of Psychology.* 2001;52: 97–422. 97

5. https://www.npr.org/2017/07/28/539726037/for-decades-these-caregivers-helped-patients-families-through-illness-and-death

CHAPTER 17

Uncertainty, Ambiguity, and DiSC®: A Contrast

They got the call just after midnight. Halfway across the country, their adult son had been ejected from a moving vehicle at high speed and was being transferred to the regional trauma center with a head injury and multiple fractures. He already was intubated, chemically paralyzed, and sedated. Immediately, their world had become uncertain, and the early messages being received were full of ambiguous commentary. Their sense that normalcy was no longer was apparent.

As physicians, regardless of our chosen discipline, we frequently embroil ourselves in our patients' lives as they learn about fresh medical uncertainty arriving unwanted. We often are the ones delivering these messages. And, unfortunately, all too often in our busyness, we occasionally forget just how deep an impact we create on people's lives — especially if we have not considered their immediate sense of uncertainty and how our own unintended delivery of ambiguous messages may contribute to it.

We need to be ever mindful that we all — patients and physicians — often carry preset expectations for how these interactions will occur when delivering or receiving difficult messages. The public media representation on healthcare delivery practices, and the stereotypes portrayed, can be a disservice to our industry at times. All too frequently, the harshness of human behavior is highlighted in both patients and care providers. Occasionally, however, the genuineness of how clinical providers interact with patients and families is more accurately rendered. These portrayals beautifully demonstrate the empathy and altruism that drive so many of us, and they also can give us personal reassurance that we are indeed privileged to be in an honorable profession.

That these portrayals also make for good "production" further emphasizes how we as humans are inherently drawn to emotionally charged situations. It is built within us all to react with genuine emotion to the complex situations of others, and for how we might help others caught in those situations. Physicians, in particular, do this well, but so do most other healthcare providers.

These stereotypes are but one example of how our preset expectations arise — for patients and for care providers. Others come from our parents, our families, our culture, our readings, and our peers.

Our industry continues to remain complex, and it will be for generations to come. At its essence, U.S. healthcare is still a free-market economy. There are numerous sectors inside the industry, including federal and state governments, that create influence of varying degree. As each sector attempts to assert its importance, pressure is exerted on the industry that may or may not have demonstrable impact. This ongoing plethora of influences is considered a positive element for any type of free market.

This plethora, however, also creates a routine, constant element of uncertainty and ambiguity for those involved in the industry.

How so? Specifically, the difficulty comes in trying to decide how or when to predict which influence (or set of influences) will create the most significant impact(s) that should be followed as an established trend that ultimately improves (or harms) industry practices.

Physicians have been focused primarily on the quickly changing trends in clinical care for several decades. We all know the rapid dissemination of medical knowledge is difficult to keep pace with, and evolving technologies make this even more complicated. Which trends in clinical care, in addition to measurement and reporting of clinical outcomes, are most relevant? Often, that is too difficult an answer to generate. The creep of uncertainty and ambiguity starts even in our cherished clinical arenas.

There are numerous studies demonstrating the dwindling morale within the physician workforce. While most physicians are happy with their career choice, the morale problems come primarily from a host of nonclinical issues and influences. Electronic health records, increased bureaucracy and overhead, dwindling compensation despite increased work hours — the list goes on, each independently and collectively compounding the sense of uncertainty and ambiguity.

The stereotype of what the profession is supposed to deliver for physicians and their lifestyles continues to change routinely. Our expectations, therefore, also must change routinely. And we all know changing expectations — after so many years of education, training and practice development — can be exceedingly difficult. However, there is some evidence out there we are indeed changing, albeit gradually.

Inherently, most physicians do not enjoy uncertainty and ambiguity. Yes, we are human, but physicians also develop certain attributes that can make accepting change even more difficult. Learning about these can help each of us deal with change better.

Psychometric profile development can be useful in several ways, and I routinely encourage people to embrace what they represent. One tool — the DiSC® profile — is used quite frequently.[1] Each letter represents a personality type within the workforce, of which there are four types (see Figure 1).

Overall, physicians tend to be quite high in the controlling characteristics related to dominance, and also fairly high in those related to conscientiousness — so much so, that I have coined a term: We tend to be a bunch of "conscientious dominators" in our professional and daily lives. Together, these two attributes alone make us want to be in control and to control the details of the situations within our environments.

DiSC® PROFILE

Dominance: Person places emphasis on accomplishing results, the bottom line, confidence:
- Sees the big picture
- Can be blunt
- Accepts challenges
- Gets straight to the point

Influence: Person places emphasis on influencing or persuading others, openness, relationships:
- Shows enthusiasm
- Is optimistic
- Likes to collaborate
- Dislikes being ignored

Steadiness: Person places emphasis on cooperation, sincerity, dependability:
- Doesn't like to be rushed
- Calm manner
- Calm approach
- Supportive actions

Conscientiousness: Person places emphasis on quality and accuracy, expertise, competency
- Enjoys independence
- Objective reasoning
- Wants the details
- Fears being wrong

FIGURE 1.

That is not an easy task in this day and age. (Interestingly, we tend to have far less orientation toward steadiness and influence — perhaps surprising, given our caring, empathetic core beliefs and behaviors.)

As you look at the listed attributes and behaviors of the DiSC® tool, you might be better able to resonate with why our industry's uncertainty and ambiguity are so unsettling at times. Understanding not only our preset expectations for situations, but also our anticipated behaviors as people, often can provide personal insights, as well as a degree of relief, on why we feel uncomfortable with our profession's changing place in the industry.

. . .

As the parents arrived at the bedside of their stricken son, it quickly became apparent to them both that normalcy for their family was gone forever. The caring, kind, and compassionate physicians and nurses were unable to easily penetrate the obvious grief of these parents. The more effort taken with communicating accurate descriptions of injuries, treatments, and prognoses, the higher their grief seemed to escalate, worsening the confusion.

Eventually, as the story unfolded, it became apparent the parents had significant health literacy problems despite a strong command of the English language. Both were naturalized citizens working hard to raise their family and to help advance the next generation. The outpouring of medical language, despite deep levels of caring, over-whelmed the capability of these parents to stay ahead of the situation, and their uncertainty led to an overwhelming feeling of ambiguity (and sense of guilt) over decisions needed for their son.

Decisions to terminate life support and proceed with organ dona-tion are never made readily by any family. And they are certainly not ones to pursue with any degree of uncertainty or ambiguity.

As physicians, we must continually seek out the uncertainty in our patients' situations and be certain for ourselves that we have not been contributing — directly or indirectly — to any ambiguity that might have crept into their situations. Personal insight and increased awareness are essential steps for achieving improved leadership, not only for those we influence, but additionally for ourselves as humans.

REFERENCE

1. https://www.discprofile.com/what-is-disc/overview/

CHAPTER 18

Diversity, Inclusion, and Physicians' Need to Give

I happened to be attending a December meeting in Manhattan on the same day as the state funeral of President George H.W. Bush in Washington, DC. New York was full of the pre-holiday joy and busyness that so many people from round the world come to seek as a rite of passage. In contrast, the ceremony for President Bush was equally global in its breadth of representation, but clearly much more somber in its purpose and intent. Both, however, created reflection on our global diversity and our ongoing needs to be more inclusive with one another as human beings.

Most of us recognize more women have been entering medical school for many years now, and the data is starting to show positive change. In 2009, the Liaison Committee on Medical Education (LCME), for one, introduced two diversity accreditation standards, mandating U.S. allopathic medical schools to engage in systematic efforts to attract and retain students from diverse backgrounds.

In a letter to *JAMA*, Dowin Boatright, MD, of Yale School of Medicine and lead researcher of a recent study on the effect of this LCME program, notes:

"From 2002 to 2009, before the standards were introduced, the proportion of women entering medical school was decreasing by 0.29 percent a year. That changed to an increase of 0.85 percent from 2012 to 2017. For African Americans, the proportions went from an annual decrease of 0.09 percent to an increase of 0.27 percent over the same time periods. Hispanic matriculation was already increasing by 0.18 percent a year in the earlier period, and almost doubled to 0.35 percent."[1]

And while there are more than 980,000 licensed U.S. physicians, according to the Federation of State Medical Boards, 30.3% of physicians are now over 60 years of age, and roughly two-thirds are male.[2] But the number of female licensed physicians has been increasing annually for the past several years.

Clearly, shifts are occurring in our professional demographics, and we all need to be prepared to accommodate these ongoing changes. So how, as leaders, do we proactively address these shifts? In his report, "What Makes a School Multicultural?,"[3] Eastern University sociologist Caleb Rosado, who specializes in diversity and multiculturalism, identifies seven important actions involved in defining multiculturalism:

- Recognizing the abundant diversity of cultures;
- Respecting the differences;
- Acknowledging the validity of different cultural expressions and contributions;
- Valuing what other cultures offer;
- Encouraging the contribution of diverse groups;
- Empowering people to strengthen themselves and others to achieve their maximum potential by being critical of their own biases; and
- Celebrating rather than just tolerating the differences in order to bring about unity through diversity.

As you consider your own personal and leadership efforts in this regard, and how best to incorporate change, here are a couple of definitions from Diversity.com to help in your reflections:

What is diversity? The short answer for the question is: "diversity and inclusive practice includes gender, religious, race, age, disability, linguistic differences, socio-economic status and cultural background."

What is inclusion? Likewise, a brief answer is: "Inclusive practice is known to be attitudes, approaches and strategies taken to make sure that students are not excluded from the learning environment because of their differences."

Giving of oneself, for me, is a core philosophy by which I recognize the ongoing need to keep giving of myself, so that I can best shift my own attitudes and approaches with others. I do this to continue improving and incorporating internal changes, to become even more inclusive of diversity in all its forms and formats. Hopefully, I keep growing as a result. This is a never-ending process of change; I encourage each of you to also move along this particular path of perpetual learning and maturing as leaders in your own organization and within your personal lives.

Thomas Nasca, MD, from the Accreditation Council for Graduate Medical Education, once told Georgetown University School of Medicine graduates, "Every patient has a 'why.' We need to listen. We need to hear it, so we can help them with the 'how,' so that they can achieve it. Your soul will be enriched by each person you care for. Pursue your calling with vigor, with commitment, with kindness, and, whenever in doubt, remember the 'why' that's in your hearts today."[4] It is a powerful message, recognizing the importance of giving that is as true for each of us promulgating leadership as it is for fresh physician graduates.

Giving of oneself also can be viewed as an uncommon form of gifting to others. While giving and gifting is too detailed a topic to cover here, Lewis Hyde's book *The Gift* provides a twist on the concept of gifts and giving of ourselves.[5] He writes, "It is also the case that a gift may be the actual agent of change, the bearer of new life." He talks about how the gifts within ourselves are also awakened when we experience the work of others and how they are shared. He further notes " . . . it is essential gifts are shared and kept moving within a community. This leads to increased connectivity and relationships, and transformative inspiration."

For those who might be intrigued, since Marcel Mauss' influential book *Essai sur le Don* first appeared in 1925,[6] the primary work on giving and gift exchange apparently has been within anthropology as it relates to giving among or between groups of individuals. Medical sociologists only recently have begun to emerge in their considerations of gift-giving — earlier work being done by Richard Titmuss in 1970, when he published *The Gift Relationship*, a study on how we handle human blood for transfusion.[7] For example, the British system classifies all blood as a gift, whereas the U.S. system has a mixed economy in which some blood is donated, and some is bought and sold.

An interesting side thought, perhaps: Within our scientific communities, gifts also can be viewed as coming in the form of scientific presentations, intellectual articles, and the sharing of theories within various communities. Therefore, the sciences arguably already have advanced rapidly in giving and gifting — increasing our connectivity and our communities.

At their core, physicians are compassionate, giving people who care deeply about others and give of ourselves routinely. Let your own altruism continue to surface so that all those around you are aware of the giving you provide with your gifts to humanity. It is what we do — it is our calling to help and care for others that ultimately benefits society. Accept the gifts of others in the process so that you are able to remain healthy and better balanced in your own approaches within this complex profession.

Atul Gawande, MD, a prominent surgeon in the Harvard system and former CEO of the healthcare venture formed by Amazon, Berkshire Hathaway, and JPMorgan Chase, said in a 2004 commencement speech: "The life of a doctor is an intense life. We are witnesses and servants to individual human survival. The difficulty is that we are also only humans ourselves. We cannot live simply for patients. In the end, we must live our own lives."[8]

We must live our own lives in a healthier, more-balanced fashion to minimize the untoward effects of this demanding profession. Giving of ourselves, while honorable and uplifting, can be draining at times. As Hyde suggests, a gift from others may be the actual agent of change, the bearer of new life. It is therefore acceptable to not only give, but to also receive.

REFERENCES

1. https://www.nbcnews.com/health/health-news/diversity-standards-produce-more-women-minorities-med-school-n943731
2. Young A, Chaudhry HJ, Pei X, et al. FSMB Census of Licensed Physicians in the United States, 2018. Journal of Medical Regulation. 2019;105(2);7-23. www.fsmb.org/siteassets/advocacy/publications/2018census.pdf.
3. https://red.pucp.edu.pe/ridei/files/2012/11/121116.pdf
4. https://gumc.georgetown.edu/gumc-stories/school-of-medicine-celebrates-166th-graduating-class/
5. Hyde L. *The Gift*. New York: Random House. 2007.
6. Mauss M. Essai sur le Don.1925.
7. Titmuss R. The Gift Relationship. 1970.
8. https://bulletin.facs.org/2018/12/presidential-address-for-our-patients/

CHAPTER 19

The Value of Volunteering

Volunteerism is the policy or practice of giving time or talents for charitable, educational, or other worthwhile activities, especially in your community. By definition, volunteering is an altruistic activity intended to promote goodness or improve quality of life. In return, this activity can produce a feeling of self-worth and respect. There is no financial gain involved for the individual. Volunteering is also known for skill development, socialization, and fun.

Skills-based volunteering is leveraging the specialized skills and talents of individuals to strengthen the infrastructure of nonprofits, helping them build and sustain their capacity to successfully achieve their missions. Many volunteers are specifically trained in the areas in which they work, such as medicine or education. Others serve on an as-needed basis, such as in response to a natural disaster.

Several of us were brought up in environments in which volunteering was a routine part of life; while for others, volunteering is a learned activity. Either way, the benefits are easily recognized. When you engage, it can help clarify who you are and consolidate your personal values as you contribute for the benefit of others.

You can volunteer in a health system or professional society, or you can volunteer to help with a variety of community services — local, regional, national, or international. Some would say both types of volunteerism are equal in importance, while others would make a distinction. I believe any type of volunteering holds value.

"A noble leader answers not to the trumpet calls of self-promotion, but to the hushed whispers of necessity."

— MOLLIE MARTI

"The interior joy we feel when we have done a good deed is the nourishment the soul requires. Wherever you turn, you can find someone who needs you. Even if it is a little thing, do something for which there is no pay but the privilege of doing it. Remember, you do not live in a world all of your own."

— ALBERT SCHWEITZER

When you are providing a contribution to a worthwhile endeavor, there are benefits for you as well as those you are helping. The value achieved does not need to have quantifiable parameters and should not necessarily require objective assessments from disengaged external reviewers.

I do agree, however, that there needs to be some form of data (qualitative and quantitative) available to help volunteers decide when, where, or how they can provide meaningful volunteer work. I also believe that only providing a financial contribution is not truly volunteerism. Certainly, financial contributions help create important and significant change in our society. But active participation in volunteerism means making an impact yourself and observing true change.

So what does volunteerism actually entail for a healthcare professional? This is a complex question to answer.

Traditional approaches include participating on committees, helping to develop educational courses, and engaging with thought leadership initiatives. These are all still important. Many pursue these for academic advancement, while others desire to contribute back to benefit the organization from an altruistic perspective. At the end of the day, however, both are equally important, and it is critical to recognize that a sense of community is often the primary motivating factor for everyone.

It is also engaging to learn from others when it comes to volunteerism. There are fascinating stories to share and opportunities to learn about new initiatives. Often, there is a fresh type of activity that one would never have considered if not through the simple act of sharing. Sharing and engaging with each other is where a sense of community can arise and flourish.

Is volunteering valuable? The answer is a simple "yes." Participate in what is meaningful for you and use the skills that you are best able to provide. The benefits are mutual for the receiver and the provider. Try it; you will like it.

Business Skills and Knowledge

CHAPTER 20

Demographics, Shifting Models, and Physician Leadership

B ased on statistics from the Federation of State Medical Boards, there are approximately one million licensed physicians in the U.S.[1]

With an average age of 51.5 years, 74.5% are certified by an American Board of Medical Specialties Specialty Board, and a large majority is licensed in a single state (78.4%). While two thirds of physicians are still male, the recognized changing demographic at the medical school level is now beginning to be noticed at the licensure level. And 33.1% of female physicians are less than 39 years old compared with only 19.2% of male physicians.[1]

With 30.3% of physicians now over age 60 years, up from 25.2% in 2010, there is clearly a demonstrable actuarial need for an increased supply of physicians in order to avert a physician manpower shortage in the near future.[1]

Generally consistent with previous reports it has issued, an analysis in 2019 by the Association of American Medical Colleges (AAMC) projects a shortage of between 46,900 to 121,900 physicians by 2032.[2] Much of the projected shortage and concern is related to the growing and aging population, reflecting both the increasing healthcare needs of older individuals as well as the practice patterns of aging physicians, who may work fewer hours or retire. Younger physicians, too, may be working fewer hours as they seek a better work-life balance.[2]

According to the U.S. Census Bureau, the year 2030 will mark an important demographic shift in the U.S. population, when all baby boomers (individuals born between 1946 and 1964) will be older than 65 years of age. By 2035, for the first time in U.S. history, adults 65 years and older are also projected to outnumber children under 18 years of age.[3]

Discussion and debate surrounding adequate provision of healthcare continues to escalate regarding implementation of the federal Affordable Care Act (ACA). The ACA will continue to expand coverage over the next few years. This plus an aging population further compounds the need for increased physician manpower coverage. The AAMC states that physician shortage numbers will increase to greater than 120,000 during the next 10 years.[2]

Additionally, distribution between physician generalist and specialist disciplines continues to be disproportionate and the preferences among physician choices for specialties are non-uniform in relation to population needs. There are also recognized trends in physician preference toward employed compensation arrangements and so-called controllable lifestyles. Two trends especially prevalent in younger generation physicians.[4,5]

Within the current era of these physician workforce changes and competing population health needs, however, there are significant evolving models of care delivery and financial payments. The various initiatives around Accountable Care Organizations and the move toward value-based payment (VBP) models being most notable these days. Newer models for medical homes and specialty medical homes are also gradually finding their way into the healthcare marketplace as a result of opportunities created with a changing landscape. And for all, to be competitive under value-based business models, hospitals (and practices) should build meaningful scale and scope, while also focusing on physician integration, costs, quality of care, and customer service.[6]

From my perspective, the traditional healthcare value equation of Value = Quality/Cost now clearly needs to also include, at the very least, Access and Efficiency in that equation.

$$Value = Quality/Cost + Access + Efficiency$$

And for our traditional models of health system — academic medical centers, aligned integrated systems, multi-hospital systems, rural hospitals, and stand-alone hospitals — in addition to the wide variety of physician practice models, all are necessarily included in the evolving requirements for meeting these shifting needs.[7]

Interestingly, Kaiser Health News (KHN) has reported that physician-owned hospitals continue to emerge as among the biggest winners under two programs in the health law. One rewards or penalizes hospitals based on how well they score on quality measures. The other penalizes hospitals where too many patients are readmitted after they leave.[8] There are now more than 260 hospitals owned by doctors scattered around 33 states (especially prevalent in Texas, Louisiana, Oklahoma, California and Kansas) according to Physician Hospitals of America, a trade group.[9]

Of 161 physician-owned hospitals that were eligible to participate in the health law's quality programs, 122 received extra money, and 39 lost funds, the KHN analysis shows, in contrast with other hospitals where 74% were penalized. Medicare is paying the average physician-owned hospital bonuses of 0.21% more for each patient during the fiscal year that runs through September, the analysis found. Meanwhile, the average hospital not run by doctors lost 0.30% per Medicare patient.

Past research has shown that physician-owned hospitals score highly in following basic clinical guidelines and pleasing patients — the same factors that Medicare is using to determine bonuses and penalties in its VBP program. These successes are arguably made easier by the fact that many patients come to these facilities for elective surgeries rather than emergencies, allowing for more orderly preparations than at a typical acute-care hospital.

Having spent more than 25 years of my career in academic safety-net institutions, I do not necessarily ascribe to physician-owned hospitals as the optimal model of care — and they do generate heated discussion among policymakers — but an argument can certainly be made that engagement of physicians and integration of physician leadership are critical for optimal success to occur in the development of these various evolving models. Why? Because physician leadership is able to provide deep and mature levels of insight on the clinical delivery side as well as on the administrative side within healthcare.

Among the nearly 6500 hospitals in the United States, only 235 are run by physicians, but the overall hospital quality scores are 25% higher when doctors run hospitals,[7] compared with other hospitals.[9]

Overall, the complexity for managing these various trends is therefore intuitively difficult and obviously creates many challenges. While moderating a panel at the World Health Care Congress 2013 on "Bending the Cost Curve," I appreciated there was clear recognition that while these fluxes and shifts within healthcare are complex, opportunity is still available in abundance to help create positive change. Strong common agreement with the panelists and audience was that in leveraging opportunity, care must continue to focus on being patient-centered. As well, general agreement demonstrated that all types of entities engaged with the healthcare industry must continue to invest in innovation and innovative approaches to these models and systems of care provision. Transparency of efforts, a degree of crowdsourcing on difficult problems, and an increase with proactive collaboration across sectors of the industry will also continue to emerge as important trends.

REFERENCES

1. Young A, Chaudhry HJ, Pei X, et al. FSMB Census of Licensed Physicians in the United States, 2018. *Journal of Medical Regulation.* 2019;105(2);7-23. www.fsmb.org/siteassets/advocacy/publications/2018census.pdf.

2. Association of American Medical Colleges. 2019 Update: The complexities of physician supply and demand: projections from 2017 to 2032. 2019. https://aamc-black. global.ssl.fastly.net/production/media/filer_public/31/13/3113ee5c-a038-4c16-89af-294a69826650/2019_update_-_the_complexities_of_physician_supply_and_demand_-_projections_from_2017-2032.pdf.

3. U.S. Census Bureau. Older people projected to outnumber children for first time in U.S. history. 2018. https://www.census.gov/newsroom/pressreleases/2018/cb18-41-population-projections.html.

4. AAMC. Center for Workforce Shortage Studies, 2010. https://www.aamc.org.

5. Kocher R, Sahni NR. Hospitals' race to employ physicians: the logic behind a money-losing proposition. *New Engl J Med.* 2011;364:1790-1793.

6. Healthcare Financial Management. November 2012. https://hfma.org.

7. Parker-Pope T. Should hospitals be run by doctors? Well Blog, New York Times. July 7, 2011. https://well.blogs.nytimes.com/2011/07/07/should-hospitals-be-run-by-doctors/.

8. Rau J. Doctor-owned hospitals prosper under health law. Kaiser Health News. April 12, 2013. https://khn.org/news/doctor-owned-hospitals-quality-bonuses/.

9. Goodall AH. Physician-leaders and hospital performance: is there an association? Soc Sci Med. 73(4):535-539, August 2011.

CHAPTER 21

Crisis Management and Catastrophes: Times for Learning?

In December 2019, an online search showed about 216 million results were found on Google in 0.51 seconds for "crisis management plan," about 15.8 million results were found in 0.53 seconds for "catastrophe management plan," and about 206 million results in 0.81 seconds for "disaster management plan." Clearly, any attempt to academically review a half-billion results to learn something more would be catastrophic in itself. I needed another path.

Most of us have been aware of disaster planning efforts for our medical facilities and within our office environments. We might even have something organized for our homes and families. And yet most of us also are aware of how imperfect those plans are and how poorly they might reflect the reality of any particular situation. Rehearsal and practicing help modulate those potential nuances, but every situation is different. For instance, just consider how we all react whenever a fire alarm sounds in our workplaces.

I am not going to take on the debate as to whether healthcare is in crisis mode — everyone is entitled to their opinions and viewpoints. I will state, however, that healthcare is an inherently complex industry and so it is easy for both optimistic and pessimistic viewpoints to emerge. Optimism tends to bring views for opportunity, while pessimism can bring views toward protectionism (also debatable). This complexity is a continuous opportunity for physician leadership and our profession to emerge continuously as an important influence for the industry to follow. The industry precedent is in place, and expectations for physicians to lead remain strong at multiple levels in our societies. In fact, physician leadership is now a strong market demand in many environments and communities as it relates to healthcare delivery.

As a business school guest lecturer, I was privileged to present the topic of physician leadership to a crowd of more than 200 graduate students and faculty from nonclinical disciplines related to healthcare (MHA, MPH, etc.). Looking out from the lectern, it was obvious even before I got into the message of my presentation that I was being held in high regard just because the audience knew I was a physician who had embraced leadership as a career path — humbling, for sure. The lecture went fine, the questions were poignant, and the swarm after the talk was gratifying. But my ego aside, the real learning moment for me — not the audience members — was in watching their enthusiasm to engage in our industry and their energy for wanting to help create further change in this complex set of systems. I left the event feeling optimistic about their futures, and ours as physicians, that we have a fresh generation coming into the field, and that their impact soon will be felt.

We already know that those entering medical school and residency programs continue to carry high levels of altruism and idealism. They, too, are driven to create change and, as best as possible, to make improvements beyond simple patient care. So if there is any form of crisis pending out there, it might be one where we, who are already in the workforce, are not effectively laying the groundwork for younger generations to more easily and readily succeed as they make their presence felt in the workforce. It is a necessity that we learn how to avert this form of a crisis so that our industry, our future peers, and our patients all can benefit from the effects of these individuals as well.

Let us pay attention; the younger generations have much to teach, and we all have much to learn from up-and-coming clinicians and other affiliated healthcare disciplines. Interprofessional approaches will only grow.

A crisis in workforce wellness also is present in our industry, and it is present within all disciplines — clinical and nonclinical. Our workforces are getting worn out with this industry's complexity and the difficulties with creating change in its systems. One easily can list all the changes needed and areas where innovation is required, but this will continue to take some time. For example, the current era of patient safety and quality is nearing 20 years. Have we made significant change in these areas? That, too, is debatable, but our workforces are getting tired in their efforts to keep making necessary changes. Large-scale industry change typically takes three to four generations of time. So what can we collectively learn?

I would advocate more simplicity, not more complexity, in the varying approaches to systems reengineering. There already is a robust science out there we need to embrace. We also need to further embrace the science for human-factors engineering to create significant change and to also incorporate the evolving science of behavioral decision-making in our efforts. These are only a couple of example areas, and I recognize it is far too easy to state their need versus actually implementing projects in this regard. Nonetheless, there is much to learn from these disciplines that we should consider integrating within healthcare.

Financial reform and realignment is another area where we can create learning opportunity. Finances drive the entire system, by necessity. Fortunately, payers in both the for-profit and public sectors are making efforts toward value-based care and payment. Once more, however, I would advocate for increased simplicity with the large number of financial models being trialed by various organizations. Let us learn to walk before we run with value-based care strategies and financial reform. That does not mean go slowly; it just means we should try to make success occur with simpler solutions that can be replicated before we advocate for the widespread, multiple pathways or experimental models. (Payers are guilty of these approaches.) Shotgun strategies only serve to confuse the marketplace and also create the risk for profiteering.

I encourage all of us to continue seeking deeper levels of optimism and to generate positive influence at all levels to which we are individually comfortable

And as we continue to make change in healthcare, let us not forget about the many individuals and communities who have been, and who will in the future be, affected by crises or catastrophes. At their core, all physicians are caring, compassionate people who care deeply about others. Let your own altruism and idealism surface so that others are aware all around you, so that you can help others in their moments of need during difficult times. It is what we do—it is our calling to help and care for others that benefits society.

CHAPTER 22

Transitions and Transformations — Our Choice?

"We cannot become what we need to be by remaining who or what we are."

— MAX DE PREE

O ur lives are a series of transitions, coupled with the occasional significant transformation. Successfully identified, embraced, and effectively managed, our lives may become rich and fulfilling. If not managed fruitfully, our lives may take a course toward frustration and disenchantment. Managing our expectations for success is pivotal in how we approach opportunities.

The healthcare industry is also a series of transitions coupled with occasional significant transformations. Each of us in healthcare has navigated a host of transitions in our attempts to keep pace with market forces; some of us have undergone significant personal and professional transformations in the process. To quote leadership guru Forrest Gump, "Life is like a box of chocolates. You never know what you are going to get."

As physicians, we have been able to craft or navigate the necessary large-scale transformations in healthcare by using the platform of physician leadership. Physician leadership has been linked to more profitable, higher-quality healthcare delivery at the organizational level, as well as better patient outcomes, increased provider satisfaction, decreased physician burnout, and improved performance of basic clinical skills. As the recent pandemic unmasked numerous vulnerabilities in the industry, from my perspective, the pipeline for physician leadership has never been more important. Newer and younger generations' approaches to physician leadership are sorely needed.

It takes time to create a significant transformation. Total experience management is a relatively new business strategy that aims to create a better, holistic experience for *everyone* who engages with a brand program or business offering (customers, employees, users, partners, etc.), fusing the voices of customers and employees with the ability to deliver extraordinary customer, employee, product, and brand experiences. It does this by combining four key experience disciplines:[1]

1. Customer experience (CX): How a customer interacts with and feels about a brand.
2. Employee experience (EX): How an employee interacts with and feels about their company.
3. User experience (UX): How a user interacts with and feels about a product or experience, especially in the digital realm, as well as face-to-face interactions.
4. Multi-experience (MX): How an experience is enhanced and delivered simultaneously across multiple devices, modalities, and touchpoints.

As we consider the potential of a total experience approach in healthcare, patient-centered/person-centered care, or PCC, is a priority as well. The challenge with PCC is that many systems and process changes are required across the clinical delivery systems and inside the various industry sectors before true PCC is possible. Transforming healthcare to PCC requires significant and sustained efforts over time. This is where the opportunity lies for physician leadership: leveraging the recognized platform of physician leadership to create the change needed.

Surprisingly, transformation requires only three things: recognizing what the current situation is; knowing what is needed or desired; and having the determination required to make the change. The challenge for healthcare is that we have only two of those three elements: we know who we are, and we seem to have the resolve required for real change. What we do not yet know, or have not adequately defined, is what healthcare should become during its next major transformation. We can, and must, do better on this latter point.

Transformational leadership is defined as a leadership approach that causes change in individuals and social systems. In its ideal form, it creates valuable and positive change in the followers with the end goal of developing followers into leaders.[2] Physicians are naturals for developing transformational leadership approaches within a variety of healthcare systems and processes.

Gary Yukl suggests several important aspects of successful transformational leadership:[3]

1. Develop a challenging and attractive vision with employees.
2. Tie the vision to a strategy for its achievement.
3. Develop the vision, specify, and translate it to actions.
4. Express confidence, decisiveness, and optimism about the vision and its implementation.
5. Realize the vision through small, planned steps and small successes in the path toward its full implementation.

Andrew Newberg, MD, and Mark Robert Waldman state,[4] "A single word has the power to influence the expression of genes that regulate physical and emotional stress." With enough sustained positive thought over time, changes in the parietal lobe functions occur, which result in changed perceptions of ourselves and others.[5] Viewing ourselves in a positive light trains our brains to also view others in a positive light. Thus, by keeping our thoughts and speech positive, we change not only our self-perception, but also our perception of the world around us, which ultimately enables us to change our reality, and the world, for the better.

Aaron Barnes, CEO of BRM Institute, provides examples of this reshaping of reality by using different types of words:[5]

- *Capability* instead of Process
- *Convergence* instead of Alignment
- *Shared Ownership* instead of Accountability
- *Demand Shaping* instead of Demand Management
- *Business Capabilities* instead of Services

Simply changing the words we use to express ideas creates a culture that does not single out or place blame on anyone within an organization. Rather, it "aims to *promote transparency, elevate communications,* and *appreciate individual value.*"[5] This shared positive language promotes effective communication and collaboration, which then breeds innovation, success, and organizational value.

The medical profession is viewed as a leadership profession not only by our industry, but also by general society. Consequently, the opportunity always is available to exhibit some version of transformational leadership in our practices, in our communities, in our organizations, in our volunteer activities — essentially in all aspects of our lives. We can, therefore, use this distinct privilege by speaking about healthcare in a positive way and by focusing on positive transformation rather than on negative market force transitions.

Unfortunately, current approaches to medical education and specialty training do not effectively incorporate exposure, nor training, in the various aspects of leadership development, change management, customer (patient) experience, or even practice management principles. It is largely left to the individual to develop knowledge and experience on the array of leadership strategies and tactics, how to consider the optimal approaches for transformational change at any level, and how to best ensure optimal patient experiences by facilitating a positive culture within the various care delivery environments. There remains much to be learned yet, and accomplished, but each of us has a responsibility to create the change wherever we have a scope of influence.

REFERENCES

1. Zande JV. What Is Customer Experience? CX Defined. *The Future of Commerce and Customer Engagement.* www.the-future-of-commerce.com/2019/06/13/what-is-customer-experience.
2. Transformational Leadership. www.langston.edu/sites/default/files/basic-content-files/TransformationalLeadership.pdf.
3. Yukl G. An Evaluation of Conceptual Weaknesses in Transformational and Charismatic Leadership Theories. *The Leadership Quarterly.* 1999;10(2):285–305.
4. Newberg A and Waldman MR. *Words Can Change Your Brain: 12 Conversation Strategies to Build Trust, Resolve Conflict, and Increase Intimacy.* New York, NY: Hudson Street Press; 2012.
5. Horton L. The Neuroscience Behind Our Words. *BRM Institute.* August 8, 2019. https://brm.institute/neuroscience-behind-words/.

CHAPTER 23

Moving Forward With Collaboration

or as long as I have been involved with the healthcare industry, as a patient and care provider, there has been ongoing commentary on the desperate need to improve healthcare. It seems we are continually declaring that the industry is undergoing transformation and change, always awaiting a new era of better care delivery. Without a doubt, healthcare is the most complex of industries. For an industry based predominantly on the patient-physician relationship, who better to provide expanded leadership and stewardship than the physicians who are its natural and historical leaders? But then, what am I saying here? It is time for change and improvement in healthcare (again) — just like it always is!

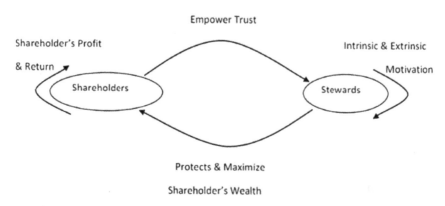

FIGURE 1. Stewardship Theory

Stewardship theory (Figure 1) assumes a humanistic model whereby steward behavior is based on serving others and will therefore align with the principal's interest. Stewardship theorists assume that given a choice between self-serving behavior and pro-organizational behavior, a steward will place a higher value on cooperation than defection. Agency theory (Figure 2), on the other hand, assumes an economic model whereby behavior is based on self-interest and may conflict with the principal's interest. An agency relationship is created when an organization (the principal) authorizes other people (agents) to act on its behalf. Governance structures that control and monitor agents are prescribed to thwart opportunistic behavior and better align the goals of the principal and agent.

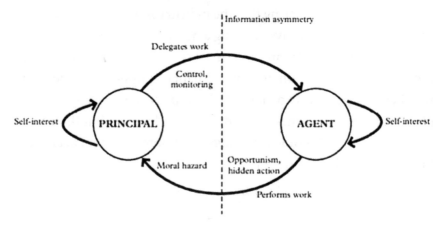

FIGURE 2. Agency Theory

Professions, generally, are designed to be self-governing and typically monitor the behaviors and outcomes of their licensed practitioners. The medical profession, in particular, has long been viewed by the public as a trusted, honorable profession that does a historically good job of educating, credentialing, monitoring, providing oversight, and self-regulating. Trust and trustworthiness in healthcare have received plenty of attention in the past few years. There was a time not long ago when patients' trust in physicians was presumed; nowadays, that level of trust and confidence appears to have eroded slightly.

However, according to a 2022 Gallup poll, nurses (79%), physicians (62%), and pharmacists (58%) are still the most highly trusted of all professions by the public.[1]

Perhaps a confluence of our historically-based professionalism is now conceptually competing with an inherent need for improved stewardship of our industry and the conflicting behaviors being exhibited throughout the industry related to that of agency theory. There likely are numerous other confounding influences at play as well. As physician leaders, we must continue learning how to better appreciate the genesis of these ever-evolving influences while also learning how to better guide their outcomes.

Paul Keckley, a brilliant healthcare economist, thought leader, and friend of physicians, in a recent posting to the *Keckley Report*, suggests physicians will indeed play a critical role in shaping the future of healthcare.[2] In his opinion, at minimum, the following issues should be considered:

- How value and affordability are defined and actualized in policies and practice.
- How the caregiver workforce is developed, composed, and evaluated based on shifting demands.
- How incentives should be set and funding sourced and rationalized across all settings and circumstances of service.
- How consumerism can be better operationalized.
- How prices and costs in every sector (including physician services) can be readily accessible.
- How a seamless system of healthcare can be built and refined.
- How physician training and performance can be modernized to participate effectively in the system's future.

Further considerations, from my perspective, are:
- American healthcare is a $4 trillion industry and represents nearly 20% of the gross domestic product.

- For a family of four, yearly healthcare expenses are now roughly $35,000, and 23% of the population experiences major unexpected medical expenses annually.
- In the United States, 23 million people (8.6%) are without health insurance in 2023, and 16% of the overall population has significant medical debt.
- Operating losses of U.S. hospitals continue at significant levels, with a third of the top 50 performers being in the red; for the top 500 hospitals, 50% are in the red.
- The healthcare industry is typically near the top of all industries in lobbying, spending millions of dollars annually to lobby the federal government — $220 million in 2022 alone.
- In the past decade, 540 physicians and more than 2,200 hospitals or healthcare companies negotiated to pay the U.S. government more than $26.8 billion in settlements or judgments related to potential criminal activity, according to Reuters.[3]

According to the Physicians Advocacy Institute, nearly 70% of American physicians are now employed in large groups, health systems, or private equity-sponsored systems.[4] The Association of American Medical Colleges (AAMC) regularly reviews the manpower of physicians, and in its most recent report suggests ongoing shortages by 2034 of between 37,800 and 124,000 physicians.[5] Clearly a shift is occurring, and, separate from the high rates of physician burnout, these shifts need to be followed closely over time.

The Department of Health and Human Services inspector general recently found that 13% of hospitalized Medicare patients experienced preventable harm during a hospital stay in October 2018.[6] A *New England Journal of Medicine* study of patients hospitalized in Massachusetts in 2018 showed that 7% had a preventable adverse event, with 1% suffering a preventable injury that was serious, life-threatening, or fatal.[7]

We all readily recognize the various statistics and could spend endless hours debating their worth or cause. Raging against the current state of affairs may serve a purpose on some level, though it typically does not create positive change in resolving issues at hand. Trying to conquer these various influences to bring healthcare systems back to historical practices is non-productive at this stage of our industry's evolution. The data already show it is not working.

Physician leadership can be, and in fact is, more than simply detailing data. Physicians are trained to be problem-solvers and to provide remedies for ailments. Embracing our professional responsibility as leaders, coupled with a renewed sense of stewardship for the industry, should capably provide the needed path forward. Numerous remedies will be required.

While I do not have all the answers, in my opinion, learning to collaborate with clinical and non-clinical cohorts in the delivery system is a necessary step forward. Physician leadership needs ways to influence healthcare in the non-clinical sectors of the industry. For example, the UnitedHealth company is now the largest employer of physicians (75,000), and it is placed among the top five Fortune 500 companies. Several other healthcare companies are also listed near the top of that list.

Physician leadership belongs to us all. Let us not waste the opportunity to collaborate more closely for the change warranted in an industry that is so deeply personal for everyone. We, our patients, and our families will all benefit from these efforts.

REFERENCES

1. Brenan M. Nurses Retain Top Ethics Rating in U.S., but Below 2020 High. Gallup. com. January 10, 2023. https://news.gallup.com/poll/467804/nurses-retain-top-ethics-rating-below-2020-high.aspx.
2. Keckley P. Special Report: Physicians on the Brink or at the Starting Line? *The Keckley Report*. May 20, 2023. https://paulkeckley.com/the-keckley-report/2023/5/30/special-report-physicians-on-the-brink-or-at-the-starting-line.

3. Berens M. How Doctors Buy Their Way Out of Trouble. *Reuters*. May 24, 2023. https://www.reuters.com/investigates/special-report/usa-healthcare-settlements.

4. Avalere Health. COVID-19's Impact on Acquisitions of Physician Practices and Physician Employment 2019-2020. *Physicians Advocacy Institute*. June 2021. https://www.physiciansadvocacyinstitute.org/Portals/0/assets/docs/Revised-6-8-21_PAI-Physician-Employment-Study-2021-FINAL.pdf.

5. The Complexities of Physician Supply and Demand: Projections From 2019 to 2034. *American Association of Medical Colleges*. Washington, DC: AAMC; June 2021. https://www.aamc.org/media/54681/download?attachment.

6. Grimm CA. *Adverse Events in Hospitals: A Quarter of Medicare Patients Experienced Harm in October 2018*. US Department of Health and Human Services, Office of Inspector General. May 2022. https://oig.hhs.gov/oei/reports/OEI-06-18-00400.pdf.

7. Bates DW, Levine DM, Salmasian J, *et al*. The Safety of Inpatient Health Care. *N Engl J Med*. 2023; 388:142–153. https://doi.org/10.1056/NEJMsa2206117.

CHAPTER 24

Diversity and Inclusion: Tough Decisions, Rich Rewards

Co-written with Andy Smith

This chapter was originally published as the cover story for the July/ August 2020 issue of Physician Leadership Journal. *All quotes are taken from a series of individual phone interviews by then-staff journalist Andy Smith.*

Consider that your organization has a diversity and inclusion program, that leadership is committed to more diversity hires, and that you are choosing between two candidates for a single job opening. Both are quality candidates, but the first clearly is more experienced and better-suited for the job. The other is a less-qualified minority applicant. Which would you hire? Which *should* you hire?

It is a common dilemma in just about every industry today, but shared angst does not make this seemingly win-lose situation any less difficult — not when you are wondering if you should lower your hiring standards in order to meet company diversity objectives.

Michellene Davis, executive vice president and chief corporate affairs officer for RWJBarnabas Health in West Orange, New Jersey, was asked a similar question at a previous job: Does diversity and inclusion mean having to lower your hiring standards? "Why in the world would you ever have to do that?" she replied. "Do you think the standards were lowered to hire me?"

No, the standards were not lowered, but Davis' status as an African-American woman had been a primary determinant in her appointment as CEO of the New Jersey Lottery in 2005. Only later did she learn that minorities had been targeted for the position and, as a board member told her, she "certainly [was] at the top of that group."

That group? What group was that? The African-American group? The women's group? Both? If the latter, she certainly checked both boxes, but the only box that mattered to Davis was the one for "most qualified." She shrugged off the awkward exchange but admits now that it inspired her to prove to them that she was undeniably "the top candidate among *any* group — not just minority, not just woman, not just minority woman."

Recently honored as one of the top 25 minority leaders by *Modern Healthcare*, Davis today supports diversity and inclusion (D&I) not as an "either/or" proposition but as a "yes/and" opportunity to identify and hire female and diverse candidates who truly are the most qualified candidates for the job. It is not a tradeoff. It is a trade-up. And it has nothing to do with hiring diverse candidates for diversity's sake.

"The first qualification is that they're highly competent," says Mark Lester, MD, MBA, CPE, FAANS, FACS, FAAPL, chairman of the board of directors for the American Association for Physician Leadership. "You don't look at someone who isn't highly competent just because they fit in an identity. That is not diversity and inclusion."

Anne Pearson, MD, CPE, senior vice president and CEO of Physicians Memorial Hermann in Houston, Texas, agrees. "I firmly believe in picking the best candidate for the job. If it's the right person and you're confident you've been objective in the interviewing and selection process, then you pick the right person for that role. The selection might not match where you think your diversity gaps are, but . . . it's not always about the identity of a specific gap; it's a more holistic approach to diversity."

If this sounds like an argument against D&I, it is not. To the contrary, D&I brings great value to an organization, its people, its culture, its patients, and its standing in the community. To get there, it helps to understand what it is, why it is important, and how to implement and sustain it.

Often lumped together, *diversity* and *inclusion* are in fact two different concepts. For example, an organization might be remarkably diverse yet not at all inclusive. Diversity and inclusion are most effective when working in tandem. Why? Because the true value of D&I comes not solely from diversity of staff but from leaders soliciting and tapping into the varied backgrounds, life experiences, and rich diversity of thought, ideas, and opinions staff members bring to an organization, representing its varied community of stakeholders. Scott E. Page, a scholar at the University of Michigan and author of *The Diversity Bonus: How Great Teams Pay Off in the Knowledge Economy*, calls this "cognitive diversity" — an expansion of thought — which is the fertile outgrowth of inclusion.

"Diversity is important, but I want to caution you: If we think that diversity is gender and race, and that by putting people of different races and genders together in an organization we have checked the diversity box and can move on, we're totally wrong," Lester insists, "because the task in diversity is broader than identity alone. The idea of diversity is integrating diverse identities and ways of thinking, creating the 'cognitive repertoire' of scholar Scott Page. And this cognitive repertoire brings much greater capacity and power than if you did not have diversity of thought."

Diversity and inclusion are complementary and essential, Lester continues, "because inclusion creates a culture where all of those diverse people can interact in a constructive and productive way, where everybody is an equal part of the team, where their contributions are recognized and respected and they can freely share them with each other." That is where the real work comes in, where leaders must exercise intentionality, consistency, perseverance, culture-building, and team-building; where understanding the lifetime of implicit bias various diversity groups faced — whether gender, race, ethnicity, sexual orientation, or religion — can optimize an organization's ability to resolve complex issues.

The reciprocal benefit, Lester adds, is that "the equity principle provides additional support for mitigating these biases with behavioral design." Behavioral design, as Iris Bohnet defines in her book *What Works: Gender Equality by Design,* is creating processes and methods that mitigate implicit bias. "Diversity and inclusion have a practical, business side when dealing with complex situations, which are predominate in healthcare," Lester says. "It also has an equity side, which means we have to do what is right and fair." That requires leadership to acknowledge and rectify past practices of inequity, including, for example, when an organization "does not have in leadership those who represent the greater microcosm of society," Davis says, adding that such initiatives cannot be achieved with words alone. It does not make a difference, for example, if a CEO says, "This is what we're doing. This is who we are," and then walks out without offering instruction or goals, leaving those in charge to their own devices.

"We're wonderfully human with all of our own implicit biases," Davis offers, "but unless you show me how, I do not know, and when the pressure is applied of trying to do more with less — as so many of us are merging and becoming these uber large organizations — our muscles atrophy. So, I return to what I've always done naturally. It's better if I understand and can grasp goals you give me, then aid me with an assessment or tools that the organization adopts to lead me through the thought process."

But again, as organizations strive to mirror the demographics of their communities, they accomplish little by hiring minorities simply to achieve diversity goals. "Having [diversity] goals is not a bad thing," Davis says, "but how you come up with your goals is important as well. You don't want to have official, role-specific mandates because then you do two things: You insult the candidate that you're hoping to secure, and you set them up for a difficult situation. I don't think it's always helpful when we're flooded with candidates who may be diverse but, quite frankly, may not have the qualifying experience. So, you're setting them up for failure, but checking off your list of diversity candidates for a search?" That's never the goal.

How many times have you attended a meeting and observed that everyone there looked pretty much the same? Davis calls that a missed opportunity, "because if you begin talking about how patients are cared for, how your service is delivered, how a new product is brought on board, about succession planning or a new hiring, but you do not have gender, racial, or ethnic diversity, then you are truly harming your organization's ability to achieve all that it can possibly do to serve all that it possibly can." If it is a missed opportunity, it is also a wake-up call to leaders to look beyond their comfort zone, beyond their network of friends and colleagues if they are truly serious about pursuing top-shelf diversity candidates.

Davis says finding such candidates is never an issue for her, but acknowledges that is not the case for many who approach her with their frustrations. Her advice: Find another search firm or alter your search methods. "I'm not trying to be funny, but why do I know so many and you seem to know none at all?" she asks them. "A lot of that deals with how we have historically placed people on boards and put them in pipelines because we socialize with them. It's who we know. You're at the club and you say to the person who was in your foursome after an enjoyable 18 holes, 'I'd love to be sitting across the table from you. Why don't you come to be on my board?'"

The problem is that networks tend to be analogous, resulting in a great deal of sameness. Her advice:

- Go online and take the Harvard Implicit Association Test (https://implicit.harvard.edu/implicit/education.html) to become aware of your own bias.
- Ensure your hiring process is as objective as possible; unquestioned subjectivity often proliferates bias.

- Understand the difference between *searching for* and *securing* diverse candidates by ensuring that the job is attractive to the candidate.

"One of the things I've heard," Davis says, "is, 'Wow, we tried to secure them, but they're asking for so much money.'" To which she answers: "And they're going to get that from someone else."

It is important to first find the most highly qualified candidates early in the recruiting process. Then, all qualifications being equal, whom do you choose? "In a situation where I'm intentionally adding to the gender diversity of my organization," Lester says, "I'm going to choose the woman. [The candidates] are equal, but I'm going to choose the woman because of the identity diversity that she'll bring to the table. You haven't made a choice to not choose someone who's more qualified. You're choosing among equally qualified people."

As a member of the search team, Davis observed that one organization for which she was conducting a search was "extremely monolithic" and she wondered why. When she asked fellow search committee members about their track record of producing diverse candidates, they indicated that they had never produced diversity candidates for that particular organization. Davis recalls: "When I asked them why, they said because that client never expressed that it was an issue of concern or desire of the organization, nor was it their aim for the ideal candidate." Another missed opportunity, she laments.

It is the same kind of missed opportunity that Barry H. Ostrowsky, president and CEO of RWJBarnabas Health, mentioned to Davis years ago, citing a clear lack of administrative diversity in the healthcare industry as a whole. Not only did Ostrowsky understand the issue, he mandated diversity components for all hiring and retention efforts, required systemwide diversity assessments for senior-level management, and empowered Davis to create internal programs for recruiting, coaching, mentoring, and sponsoring diversity candidates and staff.

The results include a program that provides paid internships for college and graduate students and recent graduates from a variety of socioeconomic backgrounds (many of whom become full-time hires), and a formal women's leadership program. Together, these in-house programs are grooming candidates and providing a sustained corporate pipeline of gender and diversity leadership. "It's not that hard," Davis says.

There is more value to these kinds of programs than just the depth of diversity leadership they provide; they also show a commitment and investment in diversity employees that goes a long way toward enhancing workplace culture and improving employee retention. "The fact that we are losing millennials to Google, Apple, and Amazon isn't just about the names Google, Apple, and Amazon," Davis argues. "It's about your most marketable, non-mainstream members leaving when they realize 'I'm in an organization that's not invested in me.' Folks are looking for a particular experience, an experience that is made better by having a diversity of thoughts and individuals who have a different type of lens through which they view the world. I call it the kaleidoscope."

Says Lester: "If we're talking about the culture that enables a team with diverse cognitive repertoires to work together and share ideas, to be constructive together, to be accepting of each other's differences, and to focus all of that in a common goal, that's a real cultural aspect. Mentoring and internal leadership programs can foster that kind of culture."

Failure to implement such programs "creates this hamster wheel of incredibly high turnover," Davis cautions. Hiring high-quality diversity candidates is the first objective, but retaining your "most marketable talent" is equally important. "The young [diversity] geniuses you hired, they're still in entry-level positions and about to hit mid-level management, but if they see everyone else around them getting mentored, coached, and sponsored and they do not receive these same career benefits — this same level of investment — then your organization is sending them a direct and succinct message, one that conveys that they are not welcome there, that they are not welcome to grow and matriculate into senior ranks," Davis says, "whether that is the intent of your message or not." Davis sounded her own message with the creation of the Young Professionals Advisory Council, which assists employees in their early- to mid-career ascension, fosters a sense of community, encourages their involvement in framing corporate culture, and makes clear the company's commitment to invest in them.

The cost of such investments is minimal compared to what Pearson describes as "the huge value in career guidance and personal development." "It really helps to have mentoring that helps you navigate a new culture or shows you the resources that are available," she says. "Even just the social factor is a huge bonus to people. For women in particular, role models can be harder to find because they're under-represented in many leadership roles. A lot of people who move into leadership have had good mentors who encouraged them along the way. I think the best mentors are maybe not similar to you; they challenge you and have different perspectives to help push the way you think about things or open you to new ideas and opportunities. That's the value of a mentor."

"When I look at the way I lead or build teams now, I'm really looking for that 'diversity bonus,'" Pearson says. "I'm looking for people's different strengths to come together, knowing that not everybody can be the best at everything and not everybody has the same background and perspective, and that finding ways that we can complement each other can really move us forward."

"Like any big initiative, it needs to be driven by leadership," she says. "They definitely have to buy into it. You have to have your senior-most executives believing that this is important and able to speak to it." Speaking to it and being intentional: making diversity hires; welcoming them to the table; encouraging them to be part of the conversation; and enabling their ascension into leadership roles.

Without that leadership support, the windfall of a "diversity bonus" is lost. "They lose out on evidence that shows that diverse work groups work harder, that they come together in a different way than a homogeneous group," Pearson says. "Obviously that bonus is an advantage to any organization that wants to be productive and move forward as far as possible. Without that, they limit their capability. In looking at how complex problems are in healthcare now, if you don't have that diversity to address the complexity, you'll struggle — and it's not going to get any easier."

It's an approach that requires team-based healthcare leaders to view diversity within the broader context of *cognitive* diversity; to recognize that identity diversity enables cognitive diversity to achieve its fullest benefit; and to value inclusion among individuals who bring their unique cognitive and identity diversity to the team in a way that ultimately achieves equity through behavioral design.

As with any initiative on the scale of diversity and inclusion, success is defined by leadership: the foresight to recognize a need for change and the fortitude to make that change happen.

Of course, it helps if you know what you are doing because "there's a huge cost if you do it wrong," warns Davis. "[Diversity and inclusion] really needs to be fostered and brought about within an organization through a design methodology," she advises, "which means that we look at it, we tweak it, we look at it again, we roll it out, we tweak it. It's got to be talked about. There's a lot of socialization that goes into it. There needs to be a communications strategy around it. And there needs to be a lot of one-on-one discussions with asset leaders across the organization because everyone needs to own a little bit of it."

The process for implementing an effective D&I program may vary from one organization to the next, but there are steps that can streamline the process and experience for all involved. D&I experts Davis, Lester, and Pearson weigh in with their own reasoned ideas.

Do an organizational assessment: Identify current gaps in identity and cognitive diversity, from the boardroom to the basement. Ask what you want to achieve and why. What is your organization and what are its priorities? If you achieve diversity and inclusion, what will that look like and what will it mean to your strategy and purpose?

Borrow ideas: Investigate what other organizations across the country are doing — both inside and outside of healthcare. "It's uber important that you not begin this work by making it up as you go along," Davis says.

Dare to compare: Compare your organization to the population you serve, then compare that to similarly situated organizations in comparably sized states. "How do they deal with an increasingly diverse population?" Davis asks. "What have they done in order to attach to them in a way that welcomes them into this space? What are some of the challenges?"

Build trust: "Your No. 1 resource is a leader or team who can get folks to trust them, who leads by example, who is collaborative and coalition-building," Davis says. "They have to have the CEO's inherent authority, shared authority . . . someone who understands that everyone comes from different spaces and places."

Empower: "Make certain you've got as many people (on board) as possible," Davis advises, "and then give them the opportunity to be leaders — to be ambassadors — to help you achieve the best-case scenario for the organization in this space."

Recognize implicit bias: "We don't want to admit that we feel certain ways that are built into us from our background and experiences and how that influences us," Pearson says, "but acknowledging bias and moving forward can be powerful. To get past that you need to put a lot of structure, processes, and leadership development into shaping an environment that mitigates bias."

Mitigate bias: A few ideas include:

1. Hide names at the tops of resumes to eliminate any unintentional first impressions that might result from "name bias."
2. After panel interviews, have panelists render decisions and offer feedback independent of each other.
3. Provide standard questions with objective scoring for each candidate so that everyone gets fair consideration. "If you ask questions based on what you need or want for a role, you don't end up talking about the fact that you both like golf," Pearson says, "because that's how interviews can veer off track." And how decisions can be swayed.

Ensure area representation: Create an advisory board of individuals who can speak for organizations that represent the demographics and backgrounds of the region. "That means going to the leader of the Hispanic Chamber of Commerce or Hispanic Bar Association as well as a local civil rights organization," Davis suggests.

Just getting the minister of the local black church is not enough, she adds. Attract individuals who have a history of experience in your region, who will make you aware of current or developing issues and concerns, and who ultimately will serve as your ambassadors.

Use internal consultants: Some organizations create a specialty position just for D&I. "If you do that, be careful you're not focused solely on demographics and identity," Lester cautions. "Demographics and identity should be a pathway to cognitive diversity, and your goal is to achieve the cognitive diversity that benefits your organization."

Lead by example: "There's something to 'seeing is believing,'" says Pearson. "Seeing someone (woman, minority) who has moved into a decision-making role can inspire others to believe that they can also contribute. That's ideal."

Garner leadership support: "What you really need is organizational leadership support to say this is important — to do this because it's the right thing to do. Otherwise, it will be a struggle unless people really believe in it and are willing to self-diagnose the issues," Pearson says.

Be intentional: Statistically speaking, the representation of women and minorities in leadership positions is proportionately less than it should be. Increasing that representation requires intentionality. "It has to be supported by leadership that is willing to allow people who think differently and challenge status quo to be at the table," Pearson says.

Be committed: Know the market demand for diversity hires and prepare yourself accordingly if you wish to secure them. "What you can't do is go to my friend, the MD from Harvard, and offer her less than what she knows you're paying," says Davis. "Highly sought-after diversity candidates know what the market demand for them is (via publicly accessible 990 forms and market research). Have a made-up mind about commitment and then follow through."

Again, for a program on the scale of diversity and inclusion, "change requires time and a great deal of training," Davis says, "but it really takes us back to what we learned in kindergarten: Treat one another as you wish to be treated."

For more: "50+ Ideas for Cultivating Diversity and Inclusion in the Workplace You Can Start Today," by Jennifer Kim: https://medium.com/@jenniferkim/50-ideas-for-cultivating-diversity-and-inclusion-in-the-workplace-you-can-start-today-fd390683bc73.

RELATED RESOURCES

What Works: Gender Equality by Design, by Iris Bohnet, Harvard Press, 2016.
The End of Diversity as We Know It: Why Diversity Efforts Fail and How Leveraging Difference Can Succeed, by Martin N. Davidson, Berrett-Koehler Publishers, 2011.
The Person You Mean to Be: How Good People Fight Bias, by Dolly Chugh, Harper Collins Publishers, 2018.

Just Medicine: A Cure for Racial Inequality in American Health Care, by Dayna Bowen Matthew, NYU Press, 2015.

The Diversity Bonus—How Great Teams Pay Off in the Knowledge Economy, by Scott E. Page, Princeton University Press, 2017.

Medical Apartheid, by Harriet A. Washington, Doubleday, 2007.

Invisible Visits, by Tina Sacks, Oxford University Press, 2019.

Blind Spot: Hidden Biases of Good People, by Mazarin R. Banji, Delacorte Press, 2013.

SECTION SIX

Leadership

CHAPTER 25

All Physicians Are Leaders
...at Some Level

All physicians are considered leaders...at some level. Whether we recognize it or not, physicians are always being looked upon in this regard. Our society certainly continues to expect the profession's members to provide representative leadership. As individuals, physicians also provide leadership within our professional, personal, and community activities on a routine basis. Leadership is what our profession has demonstrated in society for numerous generations, and it is expected to continue doing so for the foreseeable future.

With the ongoing changes in healthcare, physician leadership is now more topical and important than ever before. Regardless of whether it is formal or informal, traditional or non-traditional, one does not necessarily need to be in an organizational leadership role to provide leadership.

As one considers their evolving understanding of leadership and the potential roles they may want to explore, it is important to recognize how one's skills are viewed in the marketplace (Figure 1). Ralph Roberto of Keystone Partners once helped me appreciate the metaphor of managing your personal financial portfolio with leadership. In terms of your own career, everyone needs to regularly review their current assets and liabilities, their professional goals, a realistic time horizon, and their action plan; and certainly undergo an annual review with rebalancing of assets. In so doing, he also reiterated that

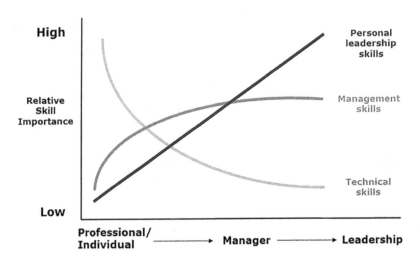

FIGURE 1. Changing Skill Requirements for Physician Leaders

the number one factor that differentiates successful leaders is their ability to gain useful feedback and then to act upon it constructively.

Physicians often miss out on the importance of taking these steps due to the busyness of their practices and not having been advised on the importance of these considerations. Figure 2 presents a useful graphic when determining the strength and relevance of your own assets as you move toward formal leadership roles, remembering, of course, that leadership also occurs without being engaged in formal positions or traditional clinical practice. It is a core of what we physicians do.

As Figure 2 depicts, leadership is the bullseye for all physicians, and moving toward that bullseye can be viewed as a gradual maturing of skills from the outer edges of the target to the inner core. Obviously this is only one depiction, and it could also be easily presented, for example, as an overlapping series of interdependent

FIGURE 2. Leadership is the Bullseye

Venn diagram circles. The overall point being, however, that we as physicians need to pay attention to these competencies as we move along our career trajectories.

And my underlying point remains: that all physicians are considered leaders at some level. Across multiple types of practice environments, physician-led healthcare provides improved outcomes, quality, safety, and efficiency. Yes, the environment of healthcare is rapidly changing, but the vast majority of healthcare is still provided under direction from physicians.

CHAPTER 26

Right-Side, Left-Side, Bi-Directional — Which is Best for Physician Leadership?

"The intuitive mind is a sacred gift, while the rational mind is a faithful servant."

— ALBERT EINSTEIN

I am right-handed for most activities, have ambidextrous talent for a few athletic activities, and often use my left hand for simpler tasks when it is easier to use than my dominant right. The dominance of one hand over the other in daily activities, however, is far different when we consider how our brains process and direct us during our routine professional activities.

I have lived a surgeon's life with strong left-brain dominance in my thinking and processing. Subsequently, I recognize how it can be problematic for me, relatively speaking, to foster a creative outlet when considering avocations. To this day, I must still ask someone for clarification on what the right side of the brain does when compared to the brain's left side. You would think having spent numerous years doing trauma surgery and looking after far too many traumatic brain injury patients that I might be able to remember.

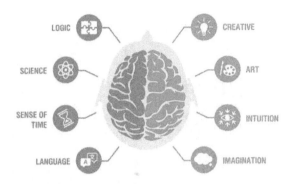

Image from https://www.simplypsychology.org/left-brain-vs-right-brain.html

Relatedly, *Doc Martin*, a popular British-based television series, follows the clinical brilliance of a surly, unemotional, and self-centered Dr. Martin Ellingham. Having developed hemophobia (fear of blood) when he starts to identify patients as humans rather than surgical cases, Ellingham, formerly an exceptionally hotshot surgeon in London, is forced to change careers, and he relocates to a small seaside town in Cornwall, UK. As a demoted urban surgeon now practicing as a rural general practitioner, he clashes with the village's quirky inhabitants, primarily because of his own highly awkward social behaviors, which seem to place him on the autism spectrum, or at least as having animotophobia (fear of emotions).

With my fairly rudimentary understanding of how the brain's two hemispheres function together, I enjoyed the series for its profiles of the extreme left-sided behavioral dominance of Ellingham, who has minimal counter-acting right-sided influences. Aside from the accurately portrayed clinical cases in the series, it is an intriguing medical drama from the perspectives of human behavior and observations on life.

In the scientifically-sound book *The Master and His Emissary*, British psychiatrist and philosopher Iain McGilchrist examines the typical manner of thinking between the right and left hemispheres of the brain. Each hemisphere provides radically different perceptions of the world. Typically, the left brain perceives the world through details, reasoning, critical thinking, and logic, while the right brain is best with creative, intuitive, and imaginative perception. Right-hemisphere thinking, with its openness to experience, plays the more important part and is a better guide to reality than the narrowly viewed, rules-based way the left hemisphere perceives the world.

So, what has all this to do with physician leadership?

The medical profession is still viewed as a leadership profession, not only by our industry, but also by general society. However, leadership is markedly different from medical practice, and there remains a paucity of exposure to leadership skill development for physicians. Medical training is designed to provide deep levels of comprehension on the many facets of pathological conditions and how best to treat them for optimal patient outcomes. This requires high levels of detail and pattern recognition, as well as critical analysis and decision-making based upon algorithmic formulae, a significant set of left-sided brain activities. Successful leadership, on the other hand, often, but not always, requires a different intellectual path of learning and knowledge processing, which, at times, relies heavily upon intuition, imagination, and strong interpersonal skills, a significant set of right-sided brain activities. Importantly, however, there is an "artful" component for both medicine and leadership whereby one must be attuned far more to the needs of others and their environments than to those needs for oneself.

McGilchrist states, "We have become enslaved to an account of things dominated by the brain's left hemisphere, one that blinds us to an awe-inspiring reality that is all around us." He suggests that to understand ourselves and the world, "we need science and intuition, together with reason and imagination."[1] Meaningful, rigorous science and reason, where both hemispheres' collective faculties are engaged, is important for a refined understanding of brain function and for moving forward in both clinical practice and physician leadership.

Each of our brain's hemispheres pays attention to the world in different ways.

When they work together, however, we perceive the whole picture of what surrounds us. According to depth psychologist Ida M. Covi, our holistic reality is ultimately based on the different kinds of attention we utilize from our left brain, our right brain, and when both hemispheres are recognized as working together. So, by using different types of attention — right, left, bi-directional — we better perceive various things, including the more beautiful and mysterious aspects of our everyday reality.[2] Thus, since our brains are involved in the making and interpretation of our entire lived experience, it is important to use our brain's collective faculties to perceive our world and to view our lives and the lives of our patients and colleagues with fresh understanding.

Therefore, as physicians, we must embrace the complexities of our industry, including brain processes. Further maximizing our inherent skills and aptitudes for clinical decision-making and leadership ability, while paying closer attention to the evolving sciences of neurobiology, neurophysiology, and psychiatry (even philosophy), can only make the care of patients better and improve the environments where we all work and recreate with others.

REFERENCES

1. McGilchrist I. *The Master and His Emissary: The Divided Brain and the Making of the Western World.* New Haven, CT: Yale University Press; 2010.
2. Covi IM. Personal communication.

CHAPTER 27

Appreciation: Where Does It Lead?

D o you still remember and appreciate the moment when you decided to enter the field of medicine or your specialty discipline, and do you fully appreciate the change in professional directions you have created for yourself over time?

Chances are you trusted some internal instincts and then corroborated those with external inputs. Or maybe you just reacted in the moment, trusting all would work out eventually. Regardless, we all can appreciate those significant moments when we changed direction.

For me, going to medical school was a presumed pathway. My parents would deny it, but there was clear bias and strong indirect influence in their counseling for me to pursue this profession. Something about "how much you intuitively care for others. . ." was the catchphrase I remember most. However, it took me many years to appreciate that they were just looking out for my best interests — according to their values.

What I better appreciate, though, is the moment I decided surgery was the optimal discipline for me. I was on a student rotation in a rural community with a small-town general surgeon. It was obvious patients loved him, other physicians respected him immensely, and he was clearly a community icon. There was something about his presence and the way he approached his work that was intangible but easy to appreciate.

Because of him, surgery itself was easy to appreciate. I intuitively learned for the first time that my thought processes and decision-making style were more compatible with surgery than with other clinical disciplines. It became a very simple choice. To this day, I appreciate the opportunity to have spent so many years in the field helping others through surgical practice.

Carl Jung once said, "With trust or loyalty to one's own experience, an individual had a solid base on which to build a life. Absent such experience, forced to rely on belief and faith, a person was liable to doubt, credulity and fear." From my perspective, trust and loyalty are an extension of appreciation of one's experiences. Continuing to acknowledge our life's trajectory, including its successes and setbacks, allows us to further appreciate how we can continue to better influence our own paths — paths that are pivotal for ongoing success as physician leaders.

So how do patients come to appreciate a physician or surgeon? What helps a leader become appreciated and trusted, enabling others to follow his or her direction with loyalty?

Sucher and Gupta penned an article in *Harvard Business Review,* "Leading with Trust."[1] They delineated how CEOs are hired " . . . to address high-stakes challenges and make tough decisions . . . their power rests on the willingness of the business's stakeholders to cede it to them . . . it depends a lot on stakeholders' trust." Five key dimensions are needed to engender ongoing trust for leaders at all levels:

1. **Legitimacy:** A leader is in that role for legitimate reasons and by a legitimate process.
2. **Competence:** A leader demonstrates skills well and is obviously good at that job.
3. **Motives:** A leader serves the interests of multiple stakeholders in a balanced fashion.
4. **Means:** A leader identifies the means needed to accomplish goals and sets the direction for an organization's actions. If those rules are perceived as fair, stakeholders will trust leaders and afford them appropriate power and loyalty.

5. **Impact:** A leader is judged on the impact created, regardless whether it was an impact that was planned or unintentional, positive or negative.

I have observed at conferences and in journals much commentary about trust — and the erosion of trust — in our industry. This is not a new topic of focus within healthcare. No doubt, we are undergoing unprecedented change, but complexity of healthcare is not a new issue, nor is the issue of whether trust is present.

Loyalty is pivotal on so many levels. Loyalty to yourself; loyalty to your family and friends; loyalty of others to you and your guidance; loyalty to your patients and patients' loyalty to you; loyalty of peers and coworkers; loyalty of your practice or organization's staff teams — the list can go on in many directions. There are volumes of research and literature on loyalty and the value it creates for individuals, patients, customers, and organizations. There even is a discipline of "loyalty-based management" that many follow. But loyalty and how it is generated is something we must all, as leaders, further understand and better appreciate for how it impacts others and our organizations.

In the corporate and association worlds, customers and members will remain loyal and keep buying or engaging only as long as they receive superior value and experiences; therefore, staff and employees must know how much value they are creating, if not individually, then as members of relatively small teams. Those in leadership must appreciate the potential for these levels of impact in either direction. These potential impacts are obvious for patient care as well.

In another significant piece, Wynia and Bedzow describe the importance of values-based leadership. In their article, "Values-Based Leadership During the Transformation of Health Care," published in *People + Strategy*, the authors describe how the changes occurring in healthcare are creating the potential for undermining healthcare's ethical foundations.[2] They posit that leaders must develop the skills necessary to give "voice" to the core values of healthcare. From their perspective, leaders must:

1. Recognize the competing ethical values underlying the challenges being faced.
2. Be competent in analyzing complex ethical dilemmas.
3. Learn to develop and implement realistic strategies that can maintain the core values of healthcare in a rapidly changing environment.

The article describes their Giving Voice to Values methodology to help leaders improve critical skills.

As individuals banding together, we can foster stronger leadership while maintaining core ethical values in addition to engendering trust and loyalty, a deeper appreciation for our past, present, and future directions. It may also enable us, as leaders of varying size teams, to better appreciate the impacts we create across an organization. These impacts on our teams most often affect patient care delivery as well as healthcare delivery — directly and indirectly. These effects are related to values, trust, and loyalty of our society in the profession and the healthcare industry as a whole.

Leadership, although complex, is often about appreciating others and how they are influenced to achieve even greater outcomes by appreciating their own potential. As you can now better recognize, appreciation in and of itself does actually lead somewhere. It helps reinforce ethical values, build trust, and engender loyalty — collectively creating value, optimizing experiences, and improving outcomes on several levels.

> "Ours is not the task of fixing the entire world all at once, but of stretching out to mend the part of the world that is within our reach. Any small, calm thing that one soul can do to help

another soul, to assist some portion of this poor suffering world, will help immensely. It is not given to us to know which acts or by whom, will cause the critical mass to tip toward an enduring good."

— CLARISSA PINKOLA ESTES
Author, poet, and psychoanalyst

REFERENCES

1. Sucher SJ, Gupta S. Leading with trust. *Harvard Business Review.* July 17, 2019. https://hbr.org/2019/07/leading-with-trust.
2. Wynia M, Bedzow I. Values-based leadership during the transformation of health care. *People + Strategy.* 2019;42(3):23-33.

CHAPTER 28

Humanism, Humility, and Physician Leadership

A s I am sure many of you did throughout the COVID-19 pandemic, I came across many examples of unhappy situations *for* others and self-centered opinions *from* others. By the same token, there were also innumerable examples of incredible acts of caring *for* others and countless illustrations of unifying, selfless behaviors *from* others.

At my core, I realized this represents how we are now living and being with the essence of human nature. Collectively, we are on a level of being human in ways we perhaps had not previously experienced or perhaps had drifted away from as a result of the routine in our daily lives. Periods in history such as this provide an opportunity to reflect on being human.

As I participate in a variety of expert panels and advisory groups, a trend I have recently noticed is the focus on solving tactical issues such as supply chain challenges, as well as expanding our focus on how we can best care for our fellow humans and how we can continue to better provide true patient-centered care. A common reflection often emerges on the essential need for strong, visionary leadership and an unwavering commitment to improving healthcare delivery practices in a more humanistic fashion.

So what is humanism? One straightforward definition is any system of thought or action that prioritizes human interests, values, and dignity. Other versions expound on secular, non-religious aspects and a lack of supernatural components. Humanist beliefs usually stress the potential value and goodness of human beings, emphasize common human needs, and seek solely rational ways of solving human problems.

Taking it further, in a May 2013 presentation on spiritual humanism to the Hangzhou International Congress, philosopher Tu Weiming stated, "A comprehensive and integrated vision for the survival and flourishing of humanity in the 21st century must take into consideration self, community, nature, and heaven as four distinct but yet interconnected dimensions of human self-understanding." He goes on to describe that as "an agenda for further exploration, spiritual humanism seeks an integration of body and mind, a fruitful interaction of self and community, a sustainable and harmonious relationship between the human species and nature, and a mutuality between the human heart and the Way of Heaven."

I prefer this latter approach to humanism because of its spiritual overlay and the added recognition of community and nature. I tend to believe that a more holistic approach to humanism is better suited to the evolving issues in our world and across our societies as a whole. While I am not an overly religious person *per se* (being primarily spiritual in focus), I recognize that religion continues to be an essential component in people's lives, regardless of the form of religion being followed; notably, all religions, irrespective of origin, carry critical components of humanism in their readings.

In an invited commentary on humanism in medicine, George Thibault states beautifully, "Humanism has been at the core of the medical profession since its inception, and it has been a foundation throughout modern history for political and community values."[1] He outlines the ways in which the efforts to humanize medicine follow the principles of humanism:

- Patients (human beings) are at the center of focus;
- Better understanding of the human experiences of both patients and clinicians are promoted;

- Professional goals and actions are derived from the real needs of patients;
- Reason is applied to better solve the problems in healthcare;
- Science is used to devise ways to better help patients maintain health.

However, if humanism is any system of thought or action that prioritizes human interests, values, and dignity, in some ways, if we are not careful, this can sound a bit like, "It's all about me." So, where does humility fit in?

Humility, it turns out, is equally challenging to synthesize simply. There is no one specific definition, and there are numerous types and attributes related to humility. It is not just about being humble! For example, some definitions state that humility requires the characteristics of self-awareness, commitment to self-improvement, appreciation for others, vision for a different future, personal integrity, and complete honesty at all times.

Neel Burton, MD, states, "Humility is more about subduing one's ego and willingly acknowledge that self-importance is less worthy of regard than group achievements."[2] Bradley Owens and David Hekman define humility as "consisting of three important pillars: a willingness to view oneself accurately, an appreciation of others' strengths and contributions, and teachability, or openness to new ideas and feedback."[3]

Don Davis and colleagues have written on distinguishing intellectual humility (IH) from general humility (GH), stating that, "GH involves (a) an accurate view of self and (b) the ability to regulate egotism and cultivate an other-oriented stance; IH is a subdomain of humility that involves (a) having an accurate view of one's intellectual strengths and limitations, and (b) the ability to negotiate ideas in a fair and inoffensive manner."[4]

Melanie Tervalon and Jann Murray-Garcia have suggested the term "cultural humility" as opposed to "cultural competency" or "cultural sensitivity" to guide clinicians in serving the needs of diverse populations.[5] Bringing attention to the internal workings of the clinician, they suggest that cultural humility is a practice committed to a lifelong process of self-evaluation and self-critique.

Sayantani DasGupta describes the concept of narrative humility: "Like the writer, whose work depends on entering into the imagined suffering of equally imagined characters, so too is the doctor intertwined inextricably with 'assumed' or 'rhetorical' suffering."[6] Within this framework, physicians witness "stories of suffering" from the perspective of narrative humility. As interviewers and witnesses, physicians "become invested in, wrapped up with," and even coauthors of their patients' "illness narratives," but we cannot ever fully comprehend another's story, "which is only ever an approximation for the totality of another's self." Therefore, DasGupta states that, "Narrative humility is a response to efforts at clinical mastery."

DasGupta suggests that narrative humility acknowledges that "our patients' stories are not objects that we can comprehend or master, but rather dynamic entities that we can approach and engage with." This engagement simultaneously requires remaining open to the stories' ambiguities and contradictions, while engaging in constant self-evaluation and self-critique regarding "our own role in the story, our expectations of the story, our responsibilities to the story, and our identifications with the story — how the story attracts or repels us because it reminds us of any number of personal stories." Through using narrative humility, she states that, "the witnessing function, so crucial to doctoring, becomes a mutual one, supporting and nourishing both individuals, while enabling a deeper, more fruitful clinical relationship."

What about leadership in this context? Traditional charismatic leadership identifies leaders through their ability to articulate a vision, empower followers to work toward achieving the vision, demonstrate charismatic behavior, and set high performance expectations for followers. The expected outcomes from this form of leadership are numerous and include increased follower motivation, enhanced follower esteem, higher performance from followers, and presumed trust in the leader. It is recognized, unfortunately, that these types of leaders often act on self-interest, exploit others, disregard others, and reject others who do not comply with the leader's agenda.

In contrast, leaders who exhibit humility and a high degree of humanism often achieve better performance results from their followers — and for their organizations. They do so by serving the collective interests of others to develop and empower followers, are follower-oriented, and tend to be altruistic in their orientation. These individuals have a socialized power motive, which reflects a concern for the group and a focus on group goals, an understanding of others, and exercising their influence for the benefit of others. Rob Nielson and colleagues contend that these types of leaders are humble in their approaches and coined the term "effective socialized charismatic leaders."[7]

The three pillars of humility from Owens and Hekman, and the importance of a leader's willingness to constantly improve and excel, incorporated with being teachable, were also identified as critical elements of humility associated with leadership by Verl Anderson and Cam Caldwell.[8] According to Edgar and Peter Schein, humble leadership is highly relational, focused on creating group trust, and based upon creating a culture that inspires everyone to collaborate to produce an optimal outcome.[9]

Pulling it all together in a meaningful context, Anatole Broyard writes: "Not every patient can be saved, but his illness may be eased by the way the doctor responds to him — and in responding to him, the doctor may save himself. But first he must become a student again; he has to dissect the cadaver of his professional persona . . . . It may be necessary to give up some of his authority in exchange for his humanity, but as the old family doctors knew, this is not a bad bargain. In learning to talk to his patients, the doctor may talk himself back into loving his work . . . by letting the sick man into his heart . . . they can share, as few others can, the wonder, terror, and exaltation of being on the edge of being, between the natural and the supernatural."[10]

In recognition that there is a robust academic knowledge-base on these topics, how does this relate to physician leadership? Physicians, by their core nature, are typically altruistic and idealistic in their beliefs. In this, a strong humanistic drive to help and care for others is usually present at a high level. The nature of the medical training paradigm, coupled with societal expectations for physicians' professional behaviors, may (at times) lead to physicians acquiring strong personality traits that do not necessarily always emulate humility. As the knowledge-base regarding effective leadership evolves, it is becoming apparent that highly effective leaders in all industries typically emulate personalities traits with higher levels of humility.

Therefore, leveraging the core altruism and humanism of physicians, and coupling this further with larger doses of humility, carries the potential for any physician to be recognized as an effective leader (formally or informally) in their community of work and personal life.

REFERENCES

1. Thibault GE. Humanism in Medicine: What Does It Mean and Why Is It More Important Than Ever? *Academic Medicine.* 2019; 94(8). doi:10.1097/ACM.0000000000002796.

2. Burton N, MD. What's the Difference Between Modesty and Humility? *Psychology Today.* https://www.psychologytoday.com/us/blog/hide-and-seek/201806/whats-the-difference-between-modesty-and-humility. Accessed November 20, 2023.

3. Owens BP and Hekman DR. How Does Leader Humility Influence Team Performance? Exploring the Mechanisms of Contagion and Collective Promotion Focus. *Academy of Management Journal.* 2015; 59(3). https://doi.org/10.5465/amj.2013.0660.

4. Davis DE, Rice K, McElroy S, et al. Distinguishing intellectual humility and general humility. *The Journal of Positive Psychology.* 2016; 11(3). https://doi.org/10.1080/17439760.2015.1048818.

5. Tervalon M and Murray-Garcia J. Cultural Humility Versus Cultural Competence: A Critical Distinction in Defining Physician Training Outcomes in Multicultural Education. *Journal of Health Care for the Poor and Underserved*. 1998; 9(2). https://doi.org/10.1353/hpu.2010.0233.

6. DasGupta S. Narrative humility. *The Lancet*. 2008; 371(9617). https://doi.org/10.1016/S0140-6736(08)60440-7.

7. Nielson R, Marrone JA, and Slay HS. A New Look at Humility: Exploring the Humility Concept and Its Role in Socialized Charismatic Leadership. *Journal of Leadership and Organizational Studies*. 2009; 17(1). https://doi.org/10.1177/1548051809350892.

8. Anderson V and Caldwell C. *Humility as Enlightened Leadership*. Hauppauge, NY: Nova Science Pub Inc; 2018.

9. Schein EH. *Organizational Culture and Leadership*. Hoboken, NJ: John Wiley & Sons; 2016.

10. Broyard A. *Intoxicated by My Illness: And Other Writings on Life and Death*. New York, NY: Clarkson Potter; 1992.

Chapter 29

Physician Leadership in Crisis and Recovery

D uring the first several months of 2020, all generations of the world's citizens witnessed or experienced what will be recognized in history as a truly monumental period of global adaptation. We all have stories about life in that yet-to-be-determined new world order. Many of us lost patients; some of us became infected ourselves. Many of our peers demonstrated profound leadership by leaning into the front lines of care; unfortunately, some also succumbed to the virus in the process.

Take a moment to pause and remember the innumerable healthcare providers from all disciplines who placed their lives at risk every day in order to help those in need during those times of overwhelming demand. If you are one of those healthcare providers, thank you for your contributions. And may all those whom we lost be remembered for their bravery.

As is apparent by the ramifications of COVID-19, our healthcare industry must continue to evolve at an ever-increasing pace despite ongoing adversity. As physicians, we routinely face adversity, but the core nature of who we are, how we were trained, and how we practice our skills help provide us with resilience. It is imperative that we continue to develop the resilience necessary to manage adversity and achieve necessary results at all levels.

"The most beautiful people we have known are those who have known defeat, known suffering, known struggle, known loss, and have found their way out of the depths. These persons have an appreciation, a sensitivity, and an understanding of life that fills them with compassion, gentleness, and a deep loving concern. Beautiful people do not just happen."[1]

— Elisabeth Kübler-Ross
On Grief & Grieving

"Resilient people do not let adversity define them. They find resilience by moving towards a goal beyond themselves, transcending pain and grief by perceiving bad times as a temporary state of affairs. . . . It's possible to strengthen your inner self and your belief in yourself, to define yourself as capable and competent. It's possible to fortify your psyche. It's possible to develop a sense of mastery."[2]

— Hara Estroff Marano
"The Art of Resilience"

During World War II, recognizing the challenge of England's ongoing fight with Germany, Winston Churchill tried to lift the spirits of the British people through a metaphor for persistence: "The nose of the bulldog is slanted backwards so he can continue to breathe without letting go." Churchill is also recognized for declaring, "We shall not fail or falter; we shall not weaken or tire. Neither the sudden shock of battle, nor the long-drawn trials of vigilance and exertion will wear us down. Give us the tools, and we will finish the job."

All physicians are viewed as leaders at some level, and often the presumption is that we have the innate ability to manage adversity effectively. Though that is not always the case, the fact that we persevered through years upon years of education to enter a career that requires persistence and resilience is a testament to our commitment. However, we must continue to develop the complex skills of resilience and persistence. Our persistence in improving resilience will lead not only to a better end result for our patients, but also to benefits for us, our families, and our communities.

> "The culture in healthcare is intricate and complex. And we know that all healthcare is ultimately local. The recent responses to COVID-19 has underscored the commitment and loyalty of our healthcare culture to providing the best of healthcare delivery to all patients in spite of the most challenging of circumstances — circumstances that often placed physicians, nurses, and other allied health providers at risk without adequate resources."

— Anonymous Physician Leader

The COVID-19 pandemic provided all of us with opportunities to learn and grow from the stories we heard about overcoming adversity — stories from patients, families, and other providers. The pride we can all feel in the way our diverse healthcare workforces came together is overwhelming, and it has become a foundational element within our healthcare culture. We were challenged, and we rose to the occasion in the most professional of self-sacrificing ways — at times with the ultimate sacrifice. Physician leadership helped drive this cultural shift.

Our society clearly benefits from the focus and skills of physicians who serve as leaders. Reflect for a moment on how strongly society has relied on physician leadership in the past few years as we navigated the public health crisis of coronavirus. Physicians were at the top echelon of influence regarding initial responses, and we continued to be at the top-tier of all health systems as each system responded in the following months. Physician leadership is critical for effective healthcare!

There is always opportunity for physicians to help initiate the changes necessary to improve our healthcare systems in the ways we so desperately desire. We must all work toward creating larger-scale change by demonstrating resilience and persistence when it comes to improving the next generation outcomes for patient care, as well as the next generation outcomes for higher quality, safer, more efficient systems of care. It is my personal commitment to physician leadership that motivates me to improve my own persistence and resilience. I do this by seeking a variety of athletic challenges, which to me represent adversity. I encourage you to find your own symbolic challenges and use persistence to develop your resilience. The culture you help create around yourself will ultimately benefit the culture around others as well.

REFERENCES

1. Kübler-Ross E, MD, Kessler D. *On Grief & Grieving: Finding the Meaning of Grief through the Five Stages of Loss.* New York, NY: Scribner; 2005.
2. Estroff Marano H. The Art of Resilience. *Psychology Today,* https://www.psychology today.com/us/articles/200305/the-art-resilience. Accessed January 5, 2024.

CHAPTER 30

We Need More Physicians Engaged With Leadership — Now!

U pon entering medical school, few of us recognized the eventual need for leadership skills. As we progressed through training, only some of us may have appreciated we were gradually inheriting leadership demands based on the patient care and treatment hierarchies in place within most clinical disciplines. Nonetheless, few of us received formal leadership education or management training in the early stages of our career education. Today, unfortunately, only a paucity of medical schools and residency programs provide a modicum of exposure to leadership development for physicians.

The healthcare industry continues to face an era of seismic change and disruption, one in which the demand for effective physician leadership is rising more dramatically than ever. The COVID-19 pandemic brought this need into sharp focus as exhausted clinicians, contentious politicians, and a terrified public cried out for leaders with medical training and priorities beyond the financial bottom line.

The demand for physician leadership is not new. Well before the pandemic's public health crisis, a constellation of forces already placed physicians at center stage. They include shifts from volume-based care delivery to a value-based system; a public health-oriented focus on the management of population wellness and resolving the multitude of social determinants of health; a new preference for person-centered care, coupled with shared decision-making; and development of safe, efficient, high-quality clinical care models in diverse settings, among many others.

Historically, healthcare delivery organizations have benefited from the distinctive perspective of physicians among their leadership. And because of increased constraints on revenue and heightened review by insurers, today's health system leaders are more often in the position of making critical administrative decisions that ultimately affect clinical care. As such, physician leaders have been described as "interface professionals" who best connect medical care with management decisions. As a bridge between other physicians, non-physician clinicians, and non-clinical administrators, physician leaders can be the catalyst that every successful organization needs, linking the so-called sharp end (the front lines of care) with the blunt end (management, leadership, and governance).

But physicians cannot do it alone, and it is not done just by doctors listening to other doctors. We must work with inter-professional clinical teams in a complex environment. Nurses, surgical technicians, nurse practitioners, physician assistants, and all other members of the healthcare team who work closely with physicians typically respect the physicians' point of view. Thus, they are more likely to buy into organizational changes and process refinements when guided or led by physicians in leadership roles.

Industry thought-leaders emphasize the critical requirement of building great teams and working within them effectively. But they also point out how challenging it can be for physicians to transition from the independent thinking driven into them during medical training to the interdependence of teamwork. We must necessarily acquire a new set of competencies, including: team building and communication skills; business intelligence in finance, marketing, strategy formulation, information technology, and law; and other knowledge needed to steer healthcare organizations of all sizes over the bumps and pitfalls of a complex system in flux.

When embracing leadership as a physician, we must all recognize this dichotomy of skills and knowledge compared to our medical training. Doing so is critically important for physicians so that success is more likely in helping, individually and collectively, to create the positive changes sorely needed in healthcare. Physicians are the expected leaders in the industry.

The literature about the benefits of physician leadership is still relatively sparse. However, a recurring illustration of the beneficial impact of physician leadership is that every year when *U.S. News & World Report's* annual "Best Hospitals Honor Roll" is reported, an overwhelming majority of top-ranked hospitals are run by physician CEOs. Others have also recently noted the strong connection between high-quality ratings and physician leadership. Another illustration is how the relationship between quality and cost creates a critical arena for collaboration among clinical and financial leaders. Effective interaction between the chief medical officer and chief financial officer requires a supporting organizational structure.

CMOs and CFOs speak different languages, have different perspectives, and focus on different goals. Clinical and financial leaders must see and understand the respective pain points of their C-suite colleagues with diverse functions. Clinical and nonclinical leaders must break down silos and establish common ground. Such collaboration is essential to increase value in healthcare and achieve success in the increasingly prevalent value-based models. Without the combined expertise of clinical and financial leaders, reaching new organizational and population health goals will be challenging, if not impossible. Encouraging clinical acumen and input with regard to operating decisions fosters collaborative work that benefits all aspects of healthcare delivery.

In light of this recognition, many hospitals and health systems are currently scrambling to recruit talented physician leader candidates from the outside. Others are grooming physician leaders internally through on-site courses, experiential learning opportunities, and certificate or advanced-degree programs with colleges and universities. Despite these efforts, they still have additional work to do in bringing more physicians into leadership.

In essence, the medical profession is still viewed as a leadership profession and our society considers all physicians to be leaders at some level. In fact, leading, and thus helping to create significant positive change, is our overall intent as physicians. Embracing the benefits of strong physician leadership can facilitate positive change in clinical care delivery and within other sectors in our industry.

And so, as physician leaders, we must embrace the complexities of our industry. We must embrace the reality we chose when transitioning to this profession. And we can choose to embrace the opportunities where our individual and collective energies are able to help create the positive transformation needed for our industry. Managing the dichotomy is essential and helping others to recognize and embrace the dichotomy is needed so that more physicians become comfortably engaged with leadership.

Note: Portions of this article appeared as an op-ed piece in Modern Healthcare *(10-3-2022)*

Growth to Move Forward — Additional Areas For Consideration

CHAPTER 31

Work and Life: Integration vs. Balance

I have two 20-something daughters whom, in mid-2021, I had not seen face-to-face in more than 18 months. Their visit over a holiday weekend was terrific and reinforced the joy of family. They did take me by surprise, though.

During one conversation, my younger daughter began sharing the array of deep thoughts she had been having about life during the past few months, and then the older one quickly offered up a series of similar comments. Both are kind, caring, and compassionate individuals who care deeply about our world and the people within, so perhaps I should not have been surprised. But I was, and it created a moment for us to more profoundly reflect about how almost everyone, at some level and regardless of age, was having similar types of thoughts. Not just thoughts about how to survive the COVID-19 pandemic, but thoughts about what they should do with their lives as a result of the pandemic's influences.

An April, 2021, *Washington Post* article states, "As the country's healthcare system has become increasingly dysfunctional in recent decades, the bulk of that dysfunction has landed on health workers — resulting in long hours, mounting paperwork and bureaucratic hurdles, fear of malpractice lawsuits and insufficient resources."[1] The article goes on to describe the personal situations for a few physicians and the changes in thought that many in healthcare were struggling to clarify for themselves. As a result, almost 30% considered leaving the industry!

Similarly, the Jackson Physician Search firm surveyed 400 physicians in late 2020, including 85 healthcare administrators who responded to questions about physician retention programs. Its white paper had five key takeaways:[2]

1. 69% of physician respondents reported being actively disengaged from employers. (The survey asked whether physicians felt engaged by their employer, whether there was effective two-way communication with administrators, and whether they had access to leadership training and career advancement to measure engagement.)

2. 54% of respondents said COVID-19 changed their employment plans.

3. Half of the respondents who planned to change their employment plans said they would consider leaving for a new employer.

4. 21% of respondents who planned to change their employment plans said they were considering early retirement.

5. 15% of respondents who planned to change their employment plans said they might leave medicine.

In a December, 2020, AMA online article, Kurt Mosley, vice president for strategic alliances at the recruiting firm Merritt Hawkins, shared that the job market for physicians had gone from a seller's market to a buyer's market and that his firm had more calls from physicians during those previous six months than they had at any time previously in recent history.[3] Before the COVID-19 pandemic, physicians' job search priorities were "sort of like real estate — it was all about location, location, location," Mosley says. "More recently, we've seen that emphasis shift to lifestyle. Now, it has become much more about what an employer can do for you. Is it a larger organization? Can they weather the storm? Can they provide child care? It's changing overnight."

We are all aware of the stress factors, increased anxieties, prevalence of burnout, and incidence of suicidality in healthcare. More recently, what has caught my attention is the number of healthcare workers who wish to leave the workforce entirely. The number who want to retire early and find nonclinical jobs and non-industry jobs seems to be escalating. Couple these data with projections for global shortages in both the physician and nursing workforces, and we have a significant potential problem for our industry — and for the care of the general population across continents.

Paradoxically, and apparently due to the pandemic, there also appears to be an increased interest by recent high school graduates to pursue healthcare across various positions and professions. After witnessing firsthand some of the horrors of illness, disability, and death so early in their lives, they have a desire to solve scientific problems, become epidemiologists or public health experts, and serve as frontline clinical providers.

The onus (in my opinion) is upon us as physician leaders to take responsibility for addressing both aspects of this paradox. We must continue to attend to the constellation of issues related to improving the wellness of our current workforce. Simultaneously, we must better prepare the existing healthcare environment to receive energetic, highly motivated, early-career stage individuals into the industry. If we do not urgently address this latter issue, we run the risk of missing a unique opportunity to leverage the motivations of a younger workforce.

Unfortunately, the industry is already at risk of not being able to keep the younger generation of healthcare workers healthy. A *Washington Post*-Kaiser Family Foundation poll of 1,327 U.S. healthcare workers in 2021 indicated that 69% of healthcare workers ages 18–29 and 61% of healthcare workers ages 30–39 indicated they felt burned out.[1]

Many of us have viewed our professional lives as separate from our personal lives. Relatively recently, there has been much talk about balancing work and life, family and friends. Unfortunately, many older workers find striking this balance difficult because they see their profession as their identity. Defining a balance is difficult and, subsequently, there is the potential for feeling like a failure if the balance is not reached.

A May, 2021, *JAMA Network Open* article addressed the issues of work-life integration in the physician workforce.[4] Although the primary outcome data focused on disparities for women in medicine, the article described the complexities of work-life balance in the overall healthcare workforce.

For many years, I have endeavored to achieve this so-called integrated work-life lifestyle. Certainly, the advent of digital devices and the ongoing expansion of technology opportunities make this lifestyle somewhat simpler. But make no mistake, you must be proactive to make this approach work — not just for yourself, but for your partner, family, and friends as well. My daughters definitely helped me.

The rise of numerous secondary influences (think telehealth, videoconferencing, remote work, etc.) is perhaps a silver lining from the COVID-19 pandemic. The existing technologies will undoubtedly continue to expand in their capabilities. The workforce across all industries will continue to explore how best to approach remote work. And our clinical delivery systems will continue to adjust to integrate telehealth as a significant portion of patient care.

Therefore, the healthcare workforce must become even more proactive with its pursuits of innovative ways that better address workforce wellness for the existing workforce and for those soon to be entering our workforce. Developing systems and processes that facilitate a simpler approach to an integrated work-life lifestyle will be imperative for many — especially the younger generations. Providing full-time dedication to the profession while still creating the risks of burnout or suicide, increasing family discourse or dissolution, or perpetuating gender or racial inequities in the workforce is an unsuccessful path. We already recognize it is unsustainable for many in these changing times.

Finding a simple balance between work and life is not so simple. Let us now think in different ways and address the opportunities at hand in a creative fashion. An integration strategy may work better, but time will tell if we begin to promulgate these approaches. Let us not miss this rare moment in history for us as physician leaders to help make this happen.

REFERENCES

1. William W. Burned out by the pandemic, 3 in 10 health-care workers consider leaving the profession. *The Washington Post*. April 22, 2021. https://www.washingtonpost.com/health/2021/04/22/health-workers-covid-quit/.

2. Stajduhar T. On the Verge of a Physician Turnover Epidemic: Physician Retention Survey Results. *Jackson Physician Search*. February 25, 2021. https://www.jacksonphysiciansearch.com/white-papers/white-paper-on-the-verge-of-a-physician-turnover-epidemic-physician-retention-survey-results/.

3. Murphy B. COVID-19 capsizes the physician job market: Trends you should know. *AMA*. December 4, 2020. https://www.ama-assn.org/medical-residents/transition-resident-attending/covid-19-capsizes-physician-job-market-trends-you.

4. Tawfik DS, Shanafelt TD, Dyrbye LN, et al. Personal and Professional Factors Associated with Work-Life Integration Among U.S. Physicians. *JAMA Netw Open*. 2021;4(5):e2111575. doi:10.1001/jamanetworkopen.2021.11575.

ADDITIONAL READING

Antonoff MB, Brown LM. Work-Life Balance: The Female Cardiothoracic Surgeon's Perspective. *J Thorac Cardiovasc Surg*. 2015;150(6):1416–21.

Baptiste D, Fecher AM, Dolejs SC, et al. Gender Differences in Academic Surgery, Work-Life Balance, and Satisfaction. *J Surg Res*. 2017;218:99–107.

Cheesborough JE, Gray SS, Bajaj AK. Striking a Better Integration of Work and Life: Challenges and Solutions. *Plast Reconstr Surg*. 2017;139(2): 495–500.

Clemen NM, Blacker BC, Floen MJ, Schweinle WE, Huber JN. Work-Life Balance in Women Physicians in South Dakota: Results of a State-Wide Assessment Survey. *S D Med*. 2018;71(12):550–58.

Dyrbye LN, Freischlag J, Kaups KL, et al. Work-Home Conflicts Have a Substantial Impact on Career Decisions That Affect the Adequacy of the Surgical Workforce. *Arch Surg*. 2012;147(10):933–39.

Dyrbye LN, Shanafelt TD, Balch CM, Satele D, Sloan J, Freischlag J. Relationship Between Work-Home Conflicts and Burnout Among American Surgeons: A Comparison By Sex. *Arch Surg.* 2011;146(2):211–17.

Dyrbye LN, Sotile W, Boone S, et al. A Survey of U.S. Physicians and Their Partners Regarding the Impact of Work-Home Conflict. *J Gen Intern Med.* 2014;29(1):155–61.

Dyrbye LN, West CP, Satele D, Sloan JA, Shanafelt TD. Work/Home Conflict and Burnout Among Academic Internal Medicine Physicians. *Arch Intern Med.* 2011;171(13):1207–09.

Garcia LC, Shanafelt TD, West CP, et al. Burnout, Depression, Career Satisfaction, and Work-Life Integration by Physician Race/Ethnicity. *JAMA Netw Open.* 2020;3(8):e2012762.

Guille C, Frank E, Zhao Z, et al. Work-family Conflict and the Sex Difference in Depression Among Training Physicians. *JAMA Intern Med.* 2017;177(12):1766–72.

Hämmig O, Brauchli R, Bauer GF. Effort-Reward and Work-Life Imbalance, General Stress and Burnout Among Employees of a Large Public Hospital in Switzerland. *Swiss Med Wkly.* 2012;142:w13577.

Huber TS. Professionalism and the Work-Life Balance. *J Vasc Surg.* 2014;60(4):1072–82.

Jolly S, Griffith KA, DeCastro R, Stewart A, Ubel P, Jagsi R. Gender Differences in Time Spent on Parenting and Domestic Responsibilities by High-Achieving Young Physician-Researchers. *Ann Intern Med.* 2014;160(5):344–53.

Kelly EL, Moen P, Tranby E. Changing Workplaces To Reduce Work-Family Conflict: Schedule Control in a White-Collar Organization. *Am Sociol Rev.* 2011;76(2):265–90.

Lin KY, Burgard SA. Working, Parenting and Work-Home Spillover: Gender Differences in the Work-Home Interface Across the Life Course. *Adv Life Course Res.* 2018;35:24–36.

Linzer M, Poplau S, Babbott S, et al. Worklife and Wellness in Academic General Internal Medicine: Results from a National Survey. *J Gen Intern Med.* 2016;31(9):1004–10.

Ly DP, Jena AB. Sex Differences in Time Spent on Household Activities and Care of Children Among US Physicians, 2003-2016. *Mayo Clin Proc.* 2018;93(10):1484–87.

Marshall AL, Dyrbye LN, Shanafelt TD, et al. Disparities in Burnout and Satisfaction with Work-Life Integration in U.S. Physicians by Gender and Practice Setting. *Acad Med.* 2020;95(9):1435–43.

Raffi J, Trivedi MK, White L, Murase JE. Work-Life Balance Among Female Dermatologists. *Int J Womens Dermatol.* 2019;6(1):13–19.

Schueller-Weidekamm C, Kautzky-Willer A. Challenges of Work-Life Balance for Women Physicians/Mothers Working in Leadership Positions. *Gend Med.* 2012;9(4):244–50.

Schwartz SP, Adair KC, Bae J, et al. Work-Life Balance Behaviours Cluster in Work Settings and Relate to Burnout and Safety Culture: A Cross-Sectional Survey Analysis. *BMJ Qual Saf.* 2019;28(2):142–50.

Sexton JB, Adair KC. Forty-Five Good Things: A Prospective Pilot Study of the Three Good Things Well-Being Intervention in the USA for Healthcare Worker Emotional Exhaustion, Depression, Work-Life Balance and Happiness. *BMJ Open.* 2019;9(3):e022695.

Sexton JB, Schwartz SP, Chadwick WA, et al. The Associations Between Work-Life Balance Behaviours, Teamwork Climate and Safety Climate: Cross-Sectional Survey Introducing The Work-Life Climate Scale, Psychometric Properties, Benchmarking Data and Future Directions. *BMJ Qual Saf.* 2017;26(8):632–40.

Shanafelt TD, Boone S, Tan L, et al. Burnout and Satisfaction with Work-Life Balance Among US Physicians Relative to the General US Population. *Arch Intern Med.* 2012;172(18):1377–85.

Shanafelt TD, Hasan O, Dyrbye LN, et al. Changes in Burnout and Satisfaction with Work-Life Balance in Physicians and the General US Working Population Between 2011 and 2014. *Mayo Clin Proc.* 2015;90(12):1600–13.

Shanafelt TD, Hasan O, Hayes S, et al. Parental Satisfaction of U.S. Physicians: Associated Factors and Comparison with the General U.S. Working Population. *BMC Med Educ.* 2016;16(1):228.

Shanafelt TD, West CP, Sinsky C, et al. Changes in Burnout and Satisfaction with Work-Life Integration in Physicians and the General US Working Population Between 2011 and 2017. *Mayo Clin Proc.* 2019;94(9):1681–94.

Sinsky CA, Dyrbye LN, West CP, Satele D, Tutty M, Shanafelt TD. Professional Satisfaction and the Career Plans of US Physicians. *Mayo Clin Proc.* 2017;92(11):1625–35.

Starmer AJ, Frintner MP, Matos K, Somberg C, Freed G, Byrne BJ. Gender Discrepancies Related to Pediatrician Work-Life Balance and Household Responsibilities. *Pediatrics.* 2019;144(4):e20182926.

Strong EA, De Castro R, Sambuco D, et al. Work-Life Balance in Academic Medicine: Narratives of Physician-Researchers and Their Mentors. *J Gen Intern Med.* 2013;28(12):1596–1603.

Chapter 32

Complementary Tensions: Desire, Ambition, Hope, and Longing

I n summer 2021, many of us hoped that our worlds would soon become clearer as the COVID-19 pandemic was presumed to be waning. I know I did. The fall brought different results, however.

What hopes had you made for yourself, your family, your practice environment, and your friends or peers? How did you have to adjust those hopes yet again?

With new hopes, renewed plans inevitably emerge for our futures. And, as I speak with many people across all generations, it seems most, at some point, have taken a degree of pause in their lives to reflect on what is truly important to them as humans in our complicated world. Emerging from these reflections, most certainly, is a recognition of whether our accumulated past experiences may, or may not, have contributed to a positive sense of well-being and whether professional or personal satisfaction is a result. For many of us, the sense of happiness is positive, but many of our peers, unfortunately, do not have a positive sense of well-being, professionally or personally.

Perhaps not surprisingly, many of these conversations with others included considerations of even larger questions, such as, "Why are we here?" and, "What's our purpose?" One went philosophical in quoting a fellow psychiatrist, Carl Jung: "The decisive question for man is: Is he related to something infinite or not? That is the telling question of his life. Only if we know that the thing which truly matters is the infinite can we avoid fixing our interests upon futilities, and upon all kinds of goals which are not of real importance."[1]

Whether you are on the positive or negative side of the well-being balance, however, there typically remains hope. Hope is all-pervasive and fuels ongoing efforts to pursue change. Coupled with hope, among an array of other diverse thoughts, feelings, and emotions, are also desires and ambitions; some of these may even reach a true sense of longing.

Interestingly, as one considers these notions, desire (at least from a definitional perspective) forms the foundation of each:[2]

- Desire – *noun* – is a strong feeling of wanting to have something or wishing for something to happen; typically, these are external and objective.
- Ambition – *noun* – is a strong desire to do or achieve something, typically requiring determination and hard work.
- Hope – *noun* – is a feeling of expectation and desire for a certain thing to happen, typically something positive and doable.
- Longing – *noun* – is a strong desire, especially for something unattainable, typically internal, and subjective.

Without getting too far into the rigorous debates of psychology or philosophy (accepting there are many) and recognizing we each already carry a unique set of ideals, values, and beliefs for how we live our lives, there is no doubt from my perspective that the complementary tensions of desire, ambition, and hope have recently been challenged in unprecedented ways.

How each of us copes and how each of us moves forward is where we differ as individuals and as professionals. Our families, patients, and practices depend heavily on how we continue to cope and adjust as physicians. Matching our ideals, values, and beliefs with our changing hopes and desires, once clarified internally, allows our natural ambitions as physicians to continue creating the needed positive changes for both our professional and personal environments. Our innate ambitions have brought each of us to our respective career stations so far, and we each have yet more to achieve individually and collectively. It remains incumbent on us to do so and to do so collaboratively within our support networks for the betterment of our industry and society as a whole.

No doubt numerous resources exist to support us in this process, such as the Greater Good Science Center at the University of California, Berkeley. It describes thirteen keys to well-being on a personal level and for a larger-scale level as well:[3]

1. Altruism
2. Awe
3. Compassion
4. Diversity
5. Empathy
6. Forgiveness
7. Gratitude
8. Happiness
9. Mindfulness
10. Purpose
11. Social Connection
12. Bridging Differences
13. Intellectual Humility

As you look at each of these key areas, recognize that, as a physician, you are already addressing each in a variety of ways. For example, compassion, empathy, altruism, purpose, and social connection are inherent to every practice environment. Diversity of patients within our environments, coupled with the awe created by the complexity of human medicine, allows us to recognize how we should be grateful and happy for the privilege of being physicians and that we should be ever mindful of the responsibility we carry for helping our fellow humans in their times of need.

And however one defines or uses forgiveness, we must also forgive ourselves for any of our past reactions or regressions secondary to the stresses of being a physician in today's environment. We must forgive to better allow ourselves to move forward with renewed hope and purpose while we re-channel our desires and ambitions.

Also from the Greater Good Science Center: ". . . forgiveness is a conscious, deliberate decision to release feelings of resentment or vengeance toward a person or group who has harmed you, regardless of whether they actually deserve your forgiveness. . . . [and while] there is some debate over whether true forgiveness requires positive feelings toward the offender, experts [do] agree that it at least involves letting go of deeply held negative feelings."[4]

I further offer that perhaps we each forgive ourselves more so than we already have as we continue to look for how to manage our sadness, anger, and possibly depression or burnout by reaching inside and drawing on our spirit, that inherent longing we all carry inside. As physicians, our healthcare industry needs us to do so, and our patients most certainly need us to do so!

So where does longing fit into this piece of our puzzle?

In their short essay "As Far As Longing Can Reach,"[5] Peter and Maria Kingsley describe longing as something far more complex than the simple definition mentioned above. For them, longing originates from the Greek *thumos*, which means "the energy of life itself. . . . the raw presence in us that senses and feels, the massed power of our emotional being." We cannot reason with our longing, we can only reason with ourselves about "the form our longing will take." Our longing "is the movement and the calling of our deepest nature," and it longs for us, as well, prompting us to become conscious. According to the Kingsleys, left to itself, longing is what allows us to "go all the way to where we really need to go." Ultimately, longing points us to "everything we need to know" about ourselves, "deep in the darkness inside ourselves." And, they argue, "if we can find the courage to face it, it will take us back to where we belong."

Brought together, the various themes in this piece are a recognition that we as physicians have so much yet to offer. Still, we need to do so by employing new and different channels or methods in leading ourselves, caring for our families, and helping those around us also to manage their hopes, desires, ambitions, and longings better.

William Carlos Williams is credited with this simple reminder:[6] "The only way to be truly happy is to make others happy." As physicians and as leaders, our desires, hopes, ambitions, and longings are often predicated on this basis: helping others live better, happier, and healthier lives.

REFERENCES

1. Jung CJ. *Memories, Dreams, Reflections* (1973). Edited by Aniela Jaffé. Translated by Richard and Clara Winston. New York, NY: Vintage Books; 1989.
2. Definitions based on *Google* search results.
3. Keys to Well-Being. *Greater Good Science Center*, https://greatergood.berkeley.edu/key. Accessed November 13, 2023.
4. Forgiveness. *Greater Good Science Center*, https://greatergood.berkeley.edu/topic/forgiveness/definition. Accessed November 13, 2023.
5. Kingsley P, Kingsley M. As Far As Longing Can Reach. *Parabola: Absence and Longing*. 2006;31(2).
6. Williams WC. 3: To His Mother. *The Selected Letters of William Carlos Williams* (1957). Edited by John C. Thirlwall. New York, NY: New Directions; 1985: 5.

CHAPTER 33

Polarity, Partisanship, and Ongoing Progress

Remember the first time you played with magnets as a child? You probably were completely mesmerized. Why did they come together in such a tight bond and then repel one another when flipped? Fascinating. Just totally fascinating!

And then some adult tried to explain to you the rationale and science behind magnetism. Do you remember their initial explanation? Nope, me neither — I was too busy playing with them to listen. In fact, I still stop to play with magnets whenever I am in a toy store or happen to see them on someone's countertop in passing.

As all of us moved through our education, regardless of the field, the concept of polarity became more evident. Science, philosophy, religion, the arts, romance, athletics — they all have components of polarity if you think about it. Good and evil, light and dark, male and female, reason and instinct, yin and yang, consciousness and unconsciousness — pairs of opposites are prevalent everywhere.

Those of us in medicine recognize how the homeostasis of our physiology depends on polarity. The host of electrolytes and their membrane exchange systems are critical and essential, simple anion-cation polarity mechanisms that help keep the majority of our *milieu intérieur* stable and balanced. So, in a general way, it is polarity that binds everything together at times. But polarity also can create strong oppositional forces at other times.

When defined as a noun, a *partisan* is an adherent or supporter of a person, group, party, or cause. *Partisanship* is the characteristic of a person who shows an especially biased, emotional allegiance, and sometimes blind adherence, to a particular person, group, party, or cause. Partisanship, therefore, can effectively represent polarity in opposite directions. When a group of like-minded partisans get together in a community to share, strong interpersonal bonds are created that provide unity of purpose and ideals. However, when a partisan group collides with other groups that hold a different sense of purpose and alternative ideals, partisanship might lead to cataclysmic outcomes.

Is this not what we continue to recognize in healthcare (let alone our federal systems): polarity and partisanship often at odds?

There is no doubt the landscape of healthcare is changing continually. The influences that are creating change come from all directions, so, predictably, certain components of partisanship and polarity arise. Intriguingly, there is always a bevy of promises for a better future in some corners and zealots claiming an impending apocalypse in other corners. Fascinating. Just totally fascinating!

Fortunately, smarter heads are prevailing in many other corners as well. Progress is being made at both the individual and the organizational levels. There always will be bell-shaped curves and references to standard deviations from the norm, but the incidence and frequency of successful efforts toward improving healthcare continue to escalate and the entire bell curve of healthcare is gradually moving forward in better directions. This is good news!

But it is also a messy business at times, and this is when leadership must provide the necessary resourcefulness to help generate an improved balance of approach. As a leader, simply asking the question, "Why can there not be approaches and benefits to a neutral or more central position?" will often reap the rewards and benefits of polarity and partisanship.

Leading is often more about deep listening — listening to others with a temporary suspension of one's personal judgment and with a willingness to receive new information. So, listening closely to the voices of polarity, while also recognizing the driving forces behind partisanship circles, often provides deeper levels of insightful information on how to achieve an improved balance of attitudes and approaches in finding new ways forward. The astute leader can then use this information and improved sense of balance among individuals of an organization to develop a new network of partisans. This new network can subsequently facilitate further change and create ongoing breakthroughs for an organization — even create a process of ongoing change management that becomes infectious on several levels.

Restating it for emphasis: Successfully concentrated, it is polarity that binds everything together at times. Not successfully concentrated, partisanship may foster strong oppositional forces that create and even nurture unproductive outcomes.

Joseph Campbell, author of *The Hero With a Thousand Faces*, in commenting on a hero's journey and how emergence across barriers is necessary for ongoing growth to occur (simplistically described as deep-level birth/rebirth experiences), stated: "The hero of yesterday becomes the tyrant of tomorrow unless he crucifies himself today."[1] The implication is that individuals, and indirectly organizations as a whole, must be cognizant of past behaviors. By doing so, they must remain open-minded toward recognizing and pursuing new approaches that are not necessarily based on premises of prior success, and that difficulties encountered in the process of change often provide deeper insights for achievements in the future. Failing to do so creates the potential for incomplete success over the longer term — an unsuccessful organizational hero journey, if you will.

Polarity is pervasive in our natural world. Partisanship is a natural tendency of human behavior. By recognizing the inevitability of both, leaders potentially can better manage the complexity of this duality to create an optimal balance for any organization to move forward constructively and successfully. Other industries harness these influences; why not ours? There clearly remains occasion for physicians to grasp the opportunities always available for creating an improved equilibrium in healthcare — our *milieu extérieur*. In fact, I believe it essential for physicians to embrace the responsibility of helping foster an improved balance between polarity and partisanship in this most complex of recognized industries.

REFERENCES

1. Campbell J. *The Hero with a Thousand Faces*, 3rd edition. Novato, CA: New World Library; 2008: 303.

CHAPTER 34

Grief, Grieving, and Grievance — Growth to Move Forward

T he loss of a cherished family member is a relatively simple, identifiable moment for each of us when grief, sadness, disbelief, and a host of other mixed emotional reactions surface to become readily recognizable. I clearly remember my first experience with death as a 12-year-old, when my grandfather passed away from advanced prostate cancer. He was a WWI veteran, wounded during the trench warfare of that era. Like many grandparents in our respective families, he was one of those revered personalities and well-loved by all. As a 12-year-old, I was quite confused but highly impressed that countless people came to his funeral. I do not, however, remember feeling sadness or other emotions related to grief. My memories are more about my curiosity about death and how people react when someone dies.

For physicians, losing a patient — or many patients during one's practice time — can create a recurring, collective sense of grief, and this accumulation gradually finds its way into our psyches in a variety of ways. Many physicians attempt to compartmentalize and bury this cumulative sense of loss (or failure as a treating physician), but there is ongoing debate as to whether this approach is beneficial or problematic to one's overall mental health and well-being. Over time, each of us ultimately finds a path that seemingly works best for us. The challenge, however, is finding a pattern of coping with this grief that does not inadvertently create long-term negative outcomes.

Recent economic challenges in healthcare, coming off the ongoing impacts of a three-year global pandemic and the profound challenges created for healthcare organizations and the clinical staff within, carry another ripe period of potential grief well beyond the often-discussed industry's clinical practice or business challenges. Helping to move the industry forward in a positive direction professionally and organizationally while attempting to overcome fresh negative impediments can seem insurmountable for many. When grief is unrecognized, untended, or not allowed to be expressed or constructively channeled, the potential for negative fallout can become manifest in a variety of ways. This outcome is already prevalent.

For example, demonstrated resilience by physicians and other clinical practitioners has been a part of their collective professional skill sets for decades. Setting expectations on the workforce for another higher level of demonstrable but poorly defined resilience may seem unrealistic to those already over-extended or overwhelmed with a cumulative sense of ennui and grief originating from a variety of sources. Facilitating constructive input from physicians to help change industry systems and processes is a better response than stating that increased resilience is a solution. So, how can we better understand our grief as physicians, and how might we convert anguish to an improved receptivity and sense for opportunity and growth?

Grief is the anguish experienced after significant loss, usually the death of a beloved one, but it may also take the form of regret for something lost, remorse for something done or not done, or sorrow for a mishap to oneself. Grief often includes physiological distress, separation anxiety, confusion, yearning, obsessive dwelling on the past, and apprehension about the future. Intense grief can become life-threatening through disruption of the immune system, self-neglect, and suicidal thoughts. These reactions can also be viewed as abnormal, traumatic, pathologic, or complicated.[1]

A recent personal discovery was Francis Weller's book *The Wild Edge of Sorrow: Rituals of Renewal and the Sacred Work of Grief.*[2] This is an intellectual treatise examining grief while also presenting rituals of renewal for better managing grief during our lifetimes. It is not a self-help book, nor does it come across as overly pedantic regarding how everyone should manage grief. Of particular interest is how the author delineates his premise on the "5 Gates of Grief." Weller offers numerous case examples while also providing insights into how different forms of ritual might be helpful. I offer my simplistic interpretation of his "5 Gates of Grief":

1. *Everything we love, we will lose.* As described above, this is the sorrow we experience with the loss of someone or something we love. Unfortunately, it is typically the only type of grief identified by current popular cultures. The catchphrase itself is an important reminder to us all, and six months of recovery for this type of loss is the norm on average.

2. *The places within that have not known love.* The events, behaviors, or emotions each of us has compartmentalized, possibly wrapped in shame, and then banished psychologically to the furthest reaches of our psyche. These neglected pieces of our personal soul ultimately are experienced as a loss within ourselves.

3. *The sorrows of the world.* The generalized sense of grief related to the current state of the world's ecology and the behaviors of its inhabitants often creates a strong sense of ill-defined loss for what is happening to the *anima mundi* (soul of the world).

4. *What we expected and did not receive.* A typically subtle grief related to not experiencing the sense of welcome, engagement, touch, and reflection originating from family, friends, and a community may commence in childhood but then be propagated in an adult, depending on individual circumstances and external influences.

5. *Ancestral grief.* The grief carried deep within us that is related to the sorrows and trials experienced by our ancestors and our heritage.

Recognizing the constellation of sources for grief and how they find their way to impacting our lives is a critical initial step. Moving forward from this recognition is an equally critical step. Grieving denotes the inner personal, psychic experience of loss and emotional pain. The grief experience comprises individual and collective thoughts, religious discourse, and subjective inner feelings about loss and psychosomatic pain.

In a complementary manner, the outward social and emotional expressions of grief embody the notion of mourning.[3] The expressions include weeping, social and religious performances in dirges and funeral rites, wistful discourse about a deceased person or entity associated with perceived loss, and ascetic actions. Consequently, mourning is influenced by one's beliefs, religious practices, and cultural context.

The oft-quoted Kübler-Ross "death and dying" grief model from 50+ years ago was developed for medical student education and was based on a series of clinical interviews with terminally ill patients. The five stages of grief identified were denial, anger, bargaining, depression, and acceptance. After initial development, it was subsequently reconceptualized in another Kübler-Ross book, *On Grief and Grieving*, from *stages* of grief to *domains* of grief, with the understanding that individuals may move back and forth among the domains without any expectation of a predefined path or progression.[4] However, Stroebe critically reviewed this model in 2017 only to find it actually had limited empirical support.[5]

Grievance is a different but related circumstance whereby one's thoughts turn to perceiving an unjust or injurious outcome creating grounds for complaint or resentment. This deeper level of grief also can take the form of a complaint or resentment within a formal statement expressed against a real or imagined wrong. In the clinical setting, these could manifest, for example, as patient complaints, medical-legal cases, or staff grievances, including burnout and discontent, submitted to a human resources department.

In the mid-'90s, one of the more promising drivers of grief or grievance recovery, beyond a normal period of grieving/mourning, emerged as the concept of post-traumatic growth (PTG): the idea that individuals can learn and draw strength from the adversities that have traumatized them. As understood by the growing field of positive psychology — a discipline that focuses on states of normalcy and happiness rather than mental and emotional dysfunction — PTG is a psychological transformation that follows a stressful encounter.[6] It is a way of finding purpose in pain and looking beyond the struggle (see Figures 1 & 2).

On the individual level, according to Jeremy Sutton, PhD, PTG can be recognized by the following positive characteristics:[6]

- The embrace of new opportunities — both on the personal and the professional fronts.
- A heightened sense of gratitude toward life altogether.
- Greater meaning and purpose.
- Increased emotional strength and resilience.
- Improved personal relationships and increased pleasure derived from being around people we love.

Choosing a path toward the benefits of positive psychology and recognizing an avenue to achieve PTG is a deeply personal matter. Francis Weller's book describes the historical importance of utilizing rituals and how to enable them in a modern world. Alternatively, simply reaching out to better connect and share with loved ones, family members, mentors, peers, or clergy members is often the easiest of initial steps. For others, engaging in individual or group therapy can hold a significant benefit as well.

While the grief may still be there, post-traumatic growth allows a person to look forward in life instead of being stuck in the past.

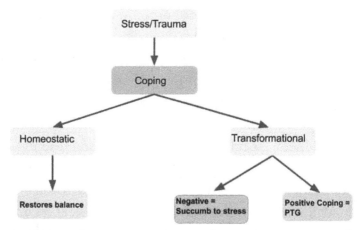

FIGURE 1. The Outcome Theory of Post-Traumatic Growth

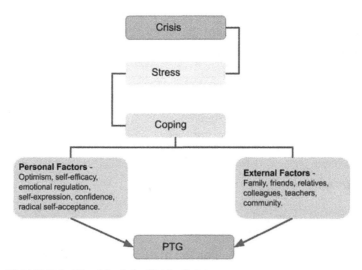

FIGURE 2. The Model of Life Crisis

Acceptance and forgiveness of oneself (but not necessarily forgetting) coupled with a personal commitment to move forward in a positive fashion is the optimal outcome.

Seeking ways to help others and the organizations where physician leadership has meaningful influence is the extrapolation of helping create post-traumatic growth for healthcare delivery, given the current industry environment. Embracing change is always important, and physician leadership has the opportunity to help reshape the evolving business of patient care delivery and the healthcare industry.

REFERENCES

1. Grief. *APA Dictionary of Psychology*. https://www.apa.org/topics/grief. Accessed January 16, 2024.
2. Weller F. *The Wild Edge of Sorrow: Rituals of Renewal and the Sacred Work of Grief.* Berkeley, CA: North Atlantic Books; 2015.
3. Mulemi BA. Mourning and Grieving. In: Leeming D. (ed) *Encyclopedia of Psychology and Religion*. Berlin: Springer; 2017. https://doi.org/10.1007/978-3-642-27771-9_9192-1.
4. Kübler-Ross E, Kessler D. *On Grief and Grieving: Finding the Meaning of Grief Through the Five Stages of Loss*. New York: Scribner; 2005.
5. Stroebe M, Schut H, Boerner K. Cautioning Healthcare Professionals: Bereaved Persons Are Misguided Through the Stages of Grief. *Omega* (Wesport). 2017;74(4):455–473. https://doi.org/10.1177/0030222817691870.
6. Sutton J. What Is Post-Traumatic Growth? (+ PTG Inventory & Scale). Positive Psychology.com. August 31, 2019. https://positivepsychology.com/post-traumatic-growth/. Accessed January 16, 2024.

CHAPTER 35

Medicine, Human Wellness, and Ecology?

A t our core, we all want to feel safe, be healthy, stay happy, and be able to live our lives with ease and minimal discomfort. In spite of other desires, at our core, these four are pivotal. Some days we forget just how privileged we are in life and become preoccupied with our unmet higher desires. Appreciating these simple core areas and purposefully choosing to be happy helps minimize the times when we feel our other wants are not being met. We often need to find supplementary activities and information to help us meet these core needs. Mounting evidence suggests that getting physically in touch with nature can improve our overall health and wellness.

The evolution of medicine as a profession and as a provision of services to people is fascinating. For centuries, the primary focus of medicine has been on the diagnosis and management of diseases. Most assuredly, the pace of change in the past 120–150 years has been spectacular, and the capabilities for providing cures (or near cures) for numerous diseases is profound. Similarly, the pace of change with the advance of scientific research breakthroughs and the development of technologies moves along at a logarithmic scale. This duplicity of change, however, makes it attractive for the science of medicine to continue focusing on disease management and not on disease prevention.

Fortunately, the past decade has shown a gradual recognition and appreciation for the need to pay more attention to human wellness and disease prevention. What began with increased attention to so-called "alternative care" practices has now evolved into a full focus on human wellness, disease prevention, and even the fast-paced new focus on longevity. These budding areas of research and product development are filled with an extensive array of confusing literature and a variety of apostles.

The general public can be misled into excess spending on products based on marginal science. Popular magazines and many books are now profiling these benefits and helping readers collate the confusing sets of scientific evidence that are spread around in a variety of research disciplines and databases — not an easy accomplishment in the least, considering at recent count, there are nearly 500 scientifically published studies from around the world linking time in nature with better health.

For example, Dr. Qing Li, a professor at the Nippon Medical School in Tokyo, has demonstrated that trees and plants emit aromatic compounds called phytoncides that, when inhaled, can spur healthy biological changes in a manner similar to aromatherapy, which also has been studied for its therapeutic benefits. In his studies, Li has shown that when people walk through or stay overnight in forests, their blood often exhibits changes that are associated with protection against cancer, improved immunity, and lower blood pressure.[1]

Specifically, Li has studied natural killer immune cells, NK cells, that, like cortisol and hemoglobin, can be reliably measured in a laboratory. It has been known for a long time that factors like stress, aging, and pesticides can reduce a person's NK count, at least temporarily. So Li wanted to learn if nature, which reduces stress, could also increase our NK cells and thereby help humans fight infections or cancer.

Li brought a group of middle-aged Tokyo businessmen into the woods in 2008. For three days, they spent a couple of hours each morning hiking. By the end of the three days, their blood tests showed their NK cells had increased 40%. Moreover, the boost lasted for seven days. A month later, their NK count was still 15% higher than when they started. In contrast, during urban walking trips of the same duration,

NK levels did not change. Li also has published results from similar studies with male and female subjects while expanding the variety and type of chemical compounds exposed to or being monitored.[2]

In a recent breakthrough study, Hunter, Gillespie, and Chen measured biomarkers of physiological stress — salivary cortisol and salivary alpha-amylase — to quantify the change in physiological stress in response to the duration of exposure to nature.[3] The use of cortisol and amylase as biomarkers is predicated on being able to separate the nature exposure effect from the natural daily shift in production.

Both stress biomarkers indicated a reduction in stress response to a "nature experience" (NE). An NE resulted in a 21.3% per hour drop in cortisol beyond that of the hormone's 11.7% diurnal drop. The NE efficiency per time expended was greatest between 20 and 30 minutes, after which benefits continued to accrue, but at a reduced rate. For salivary alpha-amylase, there was a 28.1% per hour drop after adjusting for its diurnal increase of 3.5% per hour, but only for participants who were least active, sitting or sitting with some walking. It is the first study to employ long-term, repeated-measure assessment and the first evaluation wherein study participants are free to choose the time of day, duration, and the place of an NE in response to personal preference and changing daily schedules.[3]

Building off this evolving scientific literature, Dr. Robert Zarr, a pediatrician in the Washington, DC, area, is credited with starting the nonprofit Park Rx America program (www.parkrxamerica.org) that is gradually realizing success and gaining momentum with increasing efforts to have physicians write actual prescriptions for their patients to spend time outdoors in parks close to their homes — and then facilitate their ability to do so.

Leaders like Anne O'Neill of the National Park Service and Diana Allen with the Healthy Parks Healthy People program helped launch pilot initiatives in 2011 and 2013. Many other initiatives have been, or are now becoming active, around the world as well. For example, in 2006, there was one single U.S. nature prescription program; by 2018, there were 71 programs in 32 states, and 17 states that actively use the Park Rx app.[4,5]

But here is a frustrating paradox: Morale in the healthcare workforce is under duress due to increasing pressures from increased productivity pressures, encroachment of the electronic health record, decreasing reimbursements for care, and residual debt load from training. Providers of healthcare also must pay attention to the same sets of issues with which they assist their patients; physicians must make changes to their professional and personal lives in order to be healthier. The environments where patient care is delivered also must change in order to improve the quality of life for the public and the healthcare workforce.

So how does ecology fit into this picture? The definition I found most appealing for ecology is this: " . . . it is a branch of biology that deals with the distribution, abundance and interactions of living organisms at the level of communities, populations, and ecosystems, as well as at the global scale. Ecology is a broad science encompassing many fields."[6]

But now for another disturbing paradox: When researching the topic of ecology in a variety of online databases and coupling the term to other words like "medicine," "healthcare," "physicians," etc., what do you think shows up in those searches? Unfortunately, not much of anything!

The medical profession seems to be missing the opportunity to learn more about this area of critically important knowledge. However, it is always difficult to insert new or evolving topics into the medical school curriculum; and once out of medical school, fresh graduates have myriad issues and responsibilities to address as they gain specialty training and attempt to establish their clinical practices. So frankly, it is no wonder that peripheral topics such as ecology are not included in physicians' sphere of awareness during their professional lives.

As illustrated by the example of Park Rx mentioned earlier, however, we need strategies to increase medical professionals' awareness of the rapidly escalating importance of how we are affecting ecologies and, perhaps more importantly, how our ecology can positively affect humans and those who nurture and care for them. We still have much to learn.

By nature, physicians are high achievers. At our professional core, we all want to succeed in the science and art of medicine. We also want to continue moving toward mature approaches to true patient-centered care. These professional pursuits generally provide a great sense of satisfaction. However, at times, our evolving society and medical industry do not make it easy to remain optimistic, positive, and energized. For physicians, learning how to help ourselves, and how to continue better helping others, might be reframed in the context of broader societal challenges.

It is always appealing to simplify knowledge and theory, but we must recognize that we as human beings, living on this earth within the expanding awareness of our universe, are much more complicated when it comes to health, wellness, and longevity in the face of rapidly changing ecologies. Our challenges remain to create positive change and simultaneously to continue learning as best we can about minimizing negative influences on our environments. As it turns out, keeping our lives simpler while also getting out into nature can actually provide profound benefits to our lives.

The medical profession is complex and often has difficulty adjusting to external influences beyond the sciences of traditional medical research. Yet the varieties of research outside current medical research are showing benefits to human health in a variety of ways — some quite simple, others still more complex. Consequently, medical profession education is a lifelong process of professional development that must now assimilate additional information streams into the mainstream of clinical care.

REFERENCES

1. Li Q. Effect of forest bathing trips on human immune function. *Environmental Health and Preventive Medicine* 2010;15(1):9-17.
2. Li Q. Effects of phytoncide from trees on human natural killer cell function. *International Journal of Immunopathology and Pharmacology* 2009; 22(4):951-59.
3. Hunter M, Gillespie B, Chen SY-P. Urban nature experiences reduce stress in the context of daily life based on salivary biomarkers. *Front. Psychol* 10:722. doi: 10.3389/fpsyg.2019.00722.
4. Reuben A. Ask your doctor if nature is right for you. *Outside.* May 2019.
5. Williams F. *The Nature Fix: Why Nature Makes Us Happier, Healthier, and More Creative.* New York, NY: W.W. Norton & Company; 2017.
6. Ecology. Biology Dictionary. www.biology-online.org/dictionary/ecology.

Conclusion

Engaged Physician Leadership: Current State of Affairs

As part of the American College of Healthcare Executives' 2021 annual conference, the American Association of Physician Leadership (AAPL) CEO **Peter B. Angood, MD, FRCS(C), FACS, MCCM, FAAPL(Hon),** sat down with a panel of AAPL board members to talk about engaged physician leadership and the current state of affairs. Angood spent several years as a trauma surgeon and has been in a variety of nonclinical roles, primarily within organized medicine and organized healthcare. Joining him were AAPL board chair **Mark Lester, MD, MBA, CPE, FAANS, FACS, FAAPL,** a neurosurgeon who has held several different types of leadership roles in a variety of institutions; past board chair **Greg Jolissaint, MD, MS, CPE, FAAPL,** a family medicine physician who spent many years in the military, in the VA system, and is currently part of the Trinity Healthcare System; and board member **Byron Scott, MD, MBA, CPE, FACEP, FAAPL,** an emergency medicine physician who has enjoyed a variety of roles in leadership and has been in the nonclinical arena for several years.

This transcript of their discussion has been edited for clarity and length.

PETER ANGOOD: The American Association for Physician Leadership has the philosophy that at some level, "all physicians are leaders." With that responsibility, physicians of all types, whether they have informal title roles or regular clinical roles, or even those who are outside the clinical delivery system, can be and should be effective leaders.

Given this, we thought it quite appropriate and reasonable for us to consider this current state of affairs and describe what it takes to have an engaged physician leadership. This is a dialogue. It's a conversation among four folks who have been in the trenches and have experienced lots of leadership roles.

I'm going to ask Mark Lester to kick us off.

Mark, I think you have some opinions on what engagement means, so perhaps you'll reflect on that for us.

MARK LESTER: Thanks, Peter. The title of this session is "Engaged Physician Leadership — Current State of Affairs," and I started to say to myself, "Show me a leader who is not engaged." Where else, when we talk about leadership, do we talk about the leader not being engaged? Certainly not in the political arena, certainly not in the corporate arena, certainly not in the academic world, and certainly not in healthcare.

Our leaders in healthcare are all engaged, so what are we talking about when we say we need engaged physician leadership? And what does it mean when we say that we want physician leadership engaged in the organizational improvement performance? Aren't all leaders engaged in that?

I fear that part of the issue when we discuss physician leadership is that we're kind of locked into closed-compartment thinking. In healthcare today, as it has been for over a century, the physicians in hospitals, at least, live in this animal called the "organized medical staff," and it's a relatively independent entity. It has its own bylaws, its own rules. And there are legal rules about the kinds of agreements that can be made with physicians. So already, physicians are compartmentalized at the hospital level into this medical staff organization.

When we expand broadly outside the hospital, physicians are compartmentalized into clinical thinking. Many leaders who are non-clinical think physicians only lead in a clinical space. The challenge today is that these compartments don't work as well for us because if we think about it, the biggest challenge today is to take what was classically clinical and what was classically operational and bring them together.

Isn't that why the idea of physician leadership has become so current? It's because we can't bring them together without physicians in an organization-wide leadership role. So, I think the challenge for us is not how do we engage leaders, but what's the proper model and how should we be thinking of physician leadership in healthcare today.

We are moving to pay for value. We're moving to accountable care. We're moving to real clinical integration. How does all of this work if physicians can't lead in an organizational context? I think that these questions can help us frame our conversation here.

ANGOOD: Thanks, Mark. Whenever I look at the lists of pressing issues for CEOs in healthcare delivery systems, engaging physicians is often within the top three. As the healthcare delivery system has moved along over the last couple of decades, that engagement of physicians in general is quite tricky. Is there a differentiation, then, between the regular medical staff and the physician leaders, per se?

LESTER: I would think so in terms of influence, because leadership, as distinguished from management, is all about influence. So the question is really, how do physician leaders influence their organizations and influence their nonclinical and clinical colleagues?

Remember, clinical colleagues include physicians and nurses and other healthcare staff members, so physicians who don't view themselves in an organizational leadership role may be influenced by organizational leaders, whether clinical or nonclinical. I think that can help separate what looks like a dichotomy.

ANGOOD: Right. As we know, it's that formal and informal set of relationships that often drives the culture of an organization, and that efficiency and productivity are reflected in those cultures.

Byron, the nonclinical arena has physicians in many different sectors of the industry now. How is it that physicians are engaged in some of these nonclinical sectors, and how are they viewed? Are they engaged? Are they just business people?

BYRON SCOTT: I've worked in a couple of different areas, one being technology. I also work for a consulting group, and when there's an annual employee engagement survey, everyone is lumped together, so they don't break out responses based on whether you are a physician, a nurse, or a nonclinical person. Everyone is essentially measured the same.

With that being said, when people are evaluated in the organization, especially the clinical people, [physicians] are probably viewed as engaged. This is likely based on their value to the organization and their willingness to support and help people above and beyond what their job description describes.

It's interesting when we talk about engagement. It's not necessarily separated in those types of environments. Are you just a member? Are you participating?

ANGOOD: Do you think, though, that physicians in the nonclinical sectors are held to a different standard or expectation of behavior? Or is it truly as you described: you're just like everybody else?

SCOTT: I wouldn't say you're held to a different expectation. I think everyone is held to a very high professional standard, but I think when you're a clinical person, you are probably wearing two hats. You have your employee hat, and you're expected to do certain things. But if you're a clinical person, a physician, you also have another skillset, so you're wearing a different hat. I wouldn't say it's a different expectation.

You're probably just doing two things at the same time, and you're being measured and evaluated on both.

ANGOOD: Interesting. Greg, this might not reflect my true understanding of the military and a physician in the military, but doesn't everybody in the military just follow orders? Is it easy to be engaged?

GREG JOLISSAINT: That's a great question. In combat, you follow orders. Everything outside of combat turns into using soft skills — soft skills that we want to develop in physician leaders. You can't emphasize enough the importance of communication, influence, emotional intelligence, conflict resolution, negotiation.

In the military, there is some sort of expectation that you are going to follow orders, but because at every meeting you attend, you have to convince someone that what you are trying to do for the department is good for the organization, those skills are important, even in the military.

I bounced through several federal organizations before I ended up in Trinity Health. The VA is very different in that there's no expectation that you're going to follow orders. Everything is a suggestion. And until you have said it three or four times, nobody believes you really mean it. It really does turn into a negotiation.

When it comes to the teaching hospitals, you have very few employed staff. Your staff comes from the university across the street. It's an even bigger negotiation — for example, trying to run a quality program and trying to convince the staff to be engaged in the quality program. The first goal is to negotiate to get their participation, and then they will realize the value in participating.

ANGOOD: Absolutely. If you have a healthy culture, then folks in general, whether they're physicians or other clinicians, want to help that organization move initiatives forward. Having heard all this, Mark, does that change the flavor of your comments about the generic and medical staff model or clinical delivery leaders or physicians?

LESTER: It shows that we have to move beyond just thinking about hospital structures, which were set in place in 1919 by the American College of Surgeons. That's when the organized medical staff and its bylaws were decreed in American hospitals. Nothing in healthcare is the same as it was 100 years ago, except maybe that we're in a similar pandemic now.

So, when we move beyond the strict hospital environment and we talk about physician leadership in industry, with startups, in private equity, in pharma, out in the community, and in accountable care, what we are talking about is clinical integration.

We need to be thinking about physician leadership in a generalized way. One of the things that Byron emphasized and Greg emphasized when he was talking about the military is that organizational context is vital because leadership occurs within an organizational context.

When I was with one of my organizations, I began a physician leadership development program for the entire system. It's important to teach organizational literacy because physicians tend to lack the skills. Clinical training has a different focus, and when you realize that leadership is in an organizational context and leaders have to commit themselves to that organizational context, that's when you start to think of physician leadership differently.

And you're not just thinking, "Well, they're a clinician. Maybe they can get other clinicians to do what we in the organization think is right." That really isn't the model that's going to help us moving forward.

I think what Greg and Byron said helps us generalize the idea of physician leadership and think of it in an organizational context. Then we can realize where the deficiencies in clinical training are since organizational literacy is not taught there.

ANGOOD: Absolutely. And you can go back to the old Donabedian model, where structure and process drive your outcomes. In the clinical delivery system, regardless if you have a predominantly employed physician model or you have the traditional volunteer medical staff model, one of the coveted roles that physicians often aspire to is to be on the board of that organization, thereby creating their own influence. Should physicians be on these boards? And if so, what kind of skillsets should they carry into those boards?

SCOTT: It's an interesting question, Peter, because if you go back 20–25 years ago, you probably didn't see many physicians on hospital boards and on other organization boards besides maybe a medical group. Today, there are physicians on most boards in healthcare.

But I think that like leadership development, there probably needs to be a certain skillset. Again, it's about investing in your development as a board member, because the duties of practicing clinically, having a leadership role in an organization, and being a board member are all different skill sets.

That said, I think physicians have a responsibility when they're on these healthcare boards, especially when they're with nonclinical people, because they can be a big influence. They can be the individual who can help educate nonclinical people about certain nuances. I'm a big fan of having nurses and other clinical people on boards. Either way, there needs to be the proper development and training to be involved in those roles on boards.

ANGOOD: Greg, historically, oftentimes physicians who sought out those kinds of roles would get tagged with a certain negative stigma. That may not be as prevalent these days, but given what Byron just said, as they aspire to more administrative influential roles, how do they manage that stigma?

JOLISSAINT: I think one of the things that we owe to healthcare in general is the idea of building the bench: figuring out who the next set of leaders is going to be and having those kinds of crucial conversations with them so that they understand this is not about becoming an administrator. This is not about giving orders to your peers. This is about making a difference for more than just the one patient who is sitting in front of you. This is about developing the skills that are required so that you can step back, and in a big-picture kind of format, understand where you fit into the organization, understand how to get things done in the organization, and understand how to lead in that organization.

The question is: Where is the person now in their career? Where are they regarding their leadership education? Sometimes it's just a matter of giving them the confidence by sending them to a weekend conference to develop some of these soft skills. Some of them already have it, so it's a matter of coaching them and meeting with them on a regular basis while they take over that job.

Some of them may have learned how to do spreadsheets in their formal training, but then they need to master how spreadsheets are completed in their own healthcare system or learn how to manage a budget. Filling in the gaps, from a professional basis, is going to help them be leaders.

ANGOOD: Absolutely. Mark, one of the most common questions I hear is, "Do I have to stay clinically active in order to be an effective leader inside of my healthcare delivery system?"

Personally, I've been out of clinical care now for a number of years, so perhaps my answer is a little bit artificial, but part of my message is to pay attention to your own local culture, especially around expectations. You should have the same focus and dedication to leadership expertise that you did for your clinical training and evolution. Be prepared to really invest in yourself and invest your time to be an effective, successful leader.

LESTER: If we think of leadership among physicians as strictly in the clinical space and as trying to influence other doctors to a clinical performance metric decided by an organization, that's a limited view of physician leadership.

Early in my career, I was a leader in a clinical space. Neurosurgery was a division in a department of surgery in a big tertiary medical center with a strong academic affiliation. I was able to lead both at the section level and at the department level as vice chair for operations in the department.

I don't think you need to be clinically active for many leadership roles. I'm guided by Mike Useem, who has a quote in his *The Leader's Checklists* book that says leadership is learned by practice and becomes refined and improved with practice.

By practicing leadership extensively and by devoting yourself to it, you become better at it. You continually look back, but you also look forward. When you are in a leadership role and trying to influence clinical colleagues, it's important that they see you as a credible physician. I found that the key to do this is to always relate physician-to-physician. You can do this even if you are not presently clinically active.

I think it's important for the role of physician leader or physician executive that at some point in your career, you were in the trenches clinically. With this, you understand the clinical perspective. To lead at the level that we're talking about and what's required today when we talk about accountable care, clinical integration, organizational transformation, all of these features — well, that's a full-time job. And if you're going to lead at a high level, you'll be giving clinical practice short shrift. So, I don't think it's necessary to practice clinically.

ANGOOD: I would agree with that. As I said, I've been out of clinical care a number of years, and yet I've maintained my professional association in my relevant specialties. I continue to get a variety of clinically oriented journals, and I do so because I want to be able to maintain my integrity.

Our constituency within this association is physicians of all types or multiple disciplines, a whole variety of institutional sizes and ranges. Whenever you engage with any individuals or even with some of these organizations directly, it is important to demonstrate that you're cognizant of what's going on in the healthcare industry, and to some degree what's going on in the clinical arena. Not that you need to practice, but it's maintaining that demeanor and sense of integrity as you know what it's like to be a physician. You need to be aware of the current stressors of being a physician if you are a physician leader.

Greg, with the onset of the COVID-19 pandemic, we've seen from our federal government, through the state level, and in a variety of clinical delivery systems, so-called incident crisis management assigned to teams. More often than not, it's the physicians who are in charge of those teams. And yet there are also nonclinical folks represented. The nursing perspective and pharmacist perspective are there, plus other clinical disciplines. Whether it's the hurricane, the earthquake, or the pandemic, what is the importance of incident management, and how do physicians slip into that leadership role?

JOLISSAINT: It ties back to Mark's comments about organizational literacy. When a crisis occurs, the first thing you have to decide is who's going to be most impacted by the crisis. With the pandemic, healthcare was going to be most impacted, so early on, many organizations decided to make the senior physician in the organization the incident commander. This made sense because they understood the nuances of the organization and they could step back and use the training they received (sometimes as far back as medical school) and be able to answer the public health questions that need to be addressed during a pandemic.

The physician has the ability to look across the organization and understand the impact on beds, on the nurses, the PPE, and the medical logistics. Also, transitions — what it means to transition to

12-hour shifts six days a week and the impact that that's going to have on things like resilience.

ANGOOD: Byron, you're an old emergency department sage. What's your view in terms of crisis incident management and the role of physicians as leaders in these kinds of situations?

SCOTT: I agree with Greg: You need to have senior people involved in those roles, and I can't think of anyone better than one of your organization's senior physicians. But the larger issue is the strategic plan and disaster plan. If everyone goes back and reviews their disaster plans, they're going to find that some of the basics have worked, but much of the plan didn't work. Most organizations did not expect the extent of the pandemic, even though we've been talking about a pandemic for a long time. I remind people that yes, we have COVID, but we're still due for a major influenza pandemic one day. Hopefully, we learned some good lessons.

ANGOOD: In my world of trauma surgery, I couldn't agree with you more. Without the practice and at least the tabletop exercises of scenario planning you are ill-prepared. There is this concept of swarm intelligence, that somehow the swarm will figure it all out in the heat of the battle. But you shouldn't rely on that because you still need your structure. You still need your processes.

Mark, what are some of your reflections on what we're talking about here in terms of physician leadership and command central?

LESTER: We all have a tendency to think in a very linear way. You've heard over and over again during this pandemic: "Well, what's the plan? We need a plan."

I'm guided by the words of this great sage about complex adaptive systems, Mike Tyson, who famously said that everybody has a plan until they get punched in the face. You can have a plan that's set up linearly and you think you have dealt with everything and then suddenly something happens, and it's not at all like what you predicted. We see this all the time; therefore, we have to be able to adapt and reframe our thinking.

We have to remember that we live in a fishbowl. The entire world is watching us 24/7, especially in urgent situations. You have to factor in that you are onstage continually, and your actions could be misconstrued. Communication becomes even more important in leadership in critical situations.

If we think of leadership in terms of engaging physicians so they'll do clinical things, then we're not really thinking about our world as complex adaptive systems that require physician leadership and non-clinical leadership. In the broadest sense, we need to be able to train our leaders, physicians and otherwise, to think and act in these ways.

ANGOOD: What we haven't touched on is the presence of social media in these situations. Not that the physician or the physician leader needs to engage in social media, but to your point, Mark, the healthcare delivery system is always being watched. And unfortunately, there is a section of our population that wants to engage on social media in a negative way, whether they've got the right details, the right facts, or whether they've developed misperceptions, or they're purposefully trying to create a little bit of a vicious behavior.

Should a physician leader engage with social media? Should they deflect it? Should they just let it go away? This could be a separate discussion, but I bring it up here because it is just managing the communication. Greg, what do you think?

JOLISSAINT: Hopefully, you belong to an organization that's large enough that you have people who do your marketing and communications, and you're not sitting there with your phone doing social media yourself. But social media is a powerful tool to get the information out to the public that you serve.

Whether it is messaging surrounding wearing a mask, washing your hands, and using hand sanitizer, or doing your best when your priority group comes up to be vaccinated, you can use social media to get the word out. Since everyone is being bombarded with disinformation, hopefully you and your organization have developed the rapport and integrity so the community wants to hear what you have to say. Hopefully, they are going to listen to you; they're going to act on what you say, and that's going to overcome the disinformation that's being spread in social media channels.

ANGOOD: Maybe not the social media side, but underneath all of this is data, right? And it's the flow of data, whether it's in the right channels or the wrong channels. Byron, you have experience with data and data management. How can physician leaders influence in a positive way, like Greg was just alluding to?

SCOTT: We are talking about the correct way to handle leadership, management, and communication. You need to learn how to communicate in a professional manner. Along the same lines, as a physician leader, you need to understand data and analytics. You probably need to take courses. Data can be powerful, but again, like communication, it can be misused, manipulated, or misinterpreted, so physicians need to understand where the data's coming from — can it be trusted and is it reliable? That's a skill set I think is a basic competency for physician leaders that they need to develop. This is a foundation for any healthcare leader and especially any physician leader in today's age with the speed of technology.

ANGOOD: Mark, as we think about communication and leadership, it really means we need a strong collaboration, correct? In a clinical delivery system, there's a lot of collaboration between the clinical and the nonclinical leadership, both as individuals as well as teams.

Let me ask you a two-fold question, Mark, and then we'll go over to Greg and Byron again. As you try to foster a sense of collaboration, you also encounter competition between clinical and nonclinical leadership. How do you manage that paradox of collaboration versus competition?

LESTER: I think it's a great point. We're talking about care. This is the essence of what healthcare is. Whatever we're doing in healthcare, it's about caring for people, and it's about caring for people when they're most vulnerable and most distressed and most challenged.

Care today has become very complex. Multiple pieces have to be in place and functioning properly, and often the course of a disease or an event may take a turn that wasn't anticipated. Therefore, we have to be able to rapidly recalibrate and adapt, and we have to be able to use a variety of resources. Earlier I talked about taking what was classically operational and classically clinical and joining them. You can't have those running in parallel streams today — it's too complex.

So by its nature, care mandates collaboration not only among clinicians and among non-clinicians, but also with their teams. That gets to team building. That's another piece of organizational literacy and competency physician leaders need to master. All care today is team-based, and we have to be able to collaborate and to work together.

For the idea of competition, let's look at a football team. Our organization has historically been based in Tampa, so let's look at the Tampa Bay team. You've got [Tom] Brady and [Rob Gronkowski] Gronk. They are incredible assets to that team and helped it win a Super Bowl. They may be in competition to see who can be better that day, but they're highly collaborative, so whatever competition they have is to make the team better and not to make the individuals better.

That's very important in healthcare today. It's not about the individual; it really is about the team. And that's a shift, because as a field, healthcare has always pinpointed the individual. Who could we blame for a problem? Who could we credit for a good thing? Often, when we really look, it's an entire team that produced it. The competition enhances the collaboration and enhances the team's delivery.

ANGOOD: Good points all around. And yet, Greg, we see a lot of dyad models, triad models, popping up around the country. Some of them are successful, some of them are failing, but under this same stream of collaboration–competition, what's your view from your perch?

JOLISSAINT: Comparing three different large healthcare systems, the ones that succeed understand that it's not just the nurse who's in charge of quality, and it's not just the chief medical officer who's in charge of the medical staff. They understand that it is an interdisciplinary team effort. The effort requires interdisciplinary cooperation, collegiality, and leadership. The organizations that can transition the crisis and eliminate the finger pointing are the winners. Everyone understands their role.

Yes, the physician, at the end of the day, is going to end up making the decision about the patient, but you do that with the input of the nurse who's taking care of the patient, and you're doing that with the input of the supply-chain person who tells you what equipment is working and what equipment is not working, what supplies are available and what supplies aren't available, whether it's in the ICU or in the operating room. And, by the way, if you are a true team builder, you even make the housekeeping personnel and the transporters understand their role in the care delivery system. They are part of the wellness and improvement of health of the patients in that healthcare system.

So, being able to transition a crisis means you've got to be able to have a relationship where it really is four different members of the C-suite operating in their own lanes. It is a dyad, a triad, everybody working together as a team.

ANGOOD: There's been another significant trend this past year that has caught a lot of attention, and that's healthcare equity. We tend to think about social determinants as well. It's a certain socioeconomic part of our social structure, but healthcare is not necessarily always good with equity. What is it that physician leaders and physician leadership can do to address some of these issues around equity?

SCOTT: It's been an amazing time this past year because of all the focus on health equity and health disparities in our country. Yet, this is nothing new. The health disparities that we're suddenly talking about have been there. Go back several years to the six aims of healthcare quality. One of the pillars is equitable healthcare. So, that should be a basic building block for any healthcare organization — no different than balancing the budget every month and making sure your P&L is accurate. What are you doing to measure yourself as an organization in making sure healthcare is equitable?

We all know the challenges with certain communities and social determinants of health, but again, are you doing everything you can as an organization? As a physician, I think that is one of those basic competencies, and it comes into that whole healthcare quality. I teach healthcare quality at two universities, and one of the things we focus on is those aims and making sure that people understand what equitable healthcare means and all the variants of what that means and what you need to do.

Health equity is a critical skill for physicians because if we're not taking the lead and trying to influence the organization and where it's going, that organization or others are going to be in a tough bind. While I am happy we are paying so much more attention to health equity now, we should have been doing this a long time ago.

ANGOOD: Very well said. Thank you. We don't have time to talk about all of the pros and cons of various employment models out there, but it's clear that there certainly are increased employment trends for the physician workforce. As a part of that, there's more engagement of physicians in leadership roles. Yet, some of these employment models are starting to falter and more often than not, it does come back to the communication, learning how to work together as a team, how to function in an interprofessional way.

As physicians, the way we're brought up, the way we've been trained, the way our culture pushes us along, many times we have to unlearn a lot of behaviors. Mark and I are guilty. Neurosurgeons, hard, hard egos. Trauma surgeons, probably harder egos. But both of us have had to unlearn an awful lot of behaviors in order to be successful.

That's going to be critically important in that employment arena. All of society is struggling with stress, anxiety, burnout. Suicidality is high in physicians. It's going to take a lot of systems change over a long period of time and physicians need to be engaged in order to help create these healthier environments for the workforce as a whole. In order to help us get there, Greg, do we really need all these added credentials that we've accrued behind our names? Is it important?

JOLISSAINT: It's a good question Peter, because similar to what Mark was talking about earlier, you have to bring some credibility to the table. There is a requirement that you have to demonstrate credibility as a leader. We've been talking about physician burnout for years, but I think the one thing the pandemic showed us is, it isn't just physicians who can get burned out. As soon as we as leaders of a team are able to demonstrate for our healthcare systems that we've got to worry about burnout in our nurses, we've got to worry about burnout in our respiratory therapists, this is a team sport and everybody's getting tired and everybody's getting burned out.

We've got to build resilience in the entire workforce. So yes, being able to step back as a leader and see the big picture, to see the whole organization, to understand the organization and to understand the impact of anything that the organization is going to have, it's critically important.

ANGOOD: In a few short words from each of you, and we'll start with Mark, what do you see as the future trends for increased efficiency and improvement of physician leadership in this country?

LESTER: We need to reimagine what physician leadership means and what it can bring. And then having done that, we need to provide physicians with the competencies they need. Influence, emotional intelligence, team-building, negotiation, strategic thinking, understanding operations, finance, all of these things, and understanding organizational context and what leadership means. And that means we need to work with physicians to develop their leadership for the future needs and the present needs of healthcare.

JOLISSAINT: Building the bench. Like I said earlier, we've got to identify those future leaders. We have to help them self-assess as to what their current skills are and where their gaps are. We have to help them develop the skills and tools that they're going to need in order to lead, and then we have to continue coaching them and mentoring them as they progress into the future.

At the same time, we've got to get rid of our pride and be willing to work with nurses, be willing to work with the supply-chain folks, be willing to work with the people who are going to make organizations successful. And we need to rethink the whole leadership model for healthcare systems in the first place.

SCOTT: I think it's taking all those things together and also trying to re-imagine and create innovative ways to bring joy back to work. Make work fun. I mean, medicine is hard, but all of us have had experiences where you work very hard and are very productive, but you were also having fun. And we need to make sure that no matter what, we continue to emphasize that. No matter what, let's bring that element of joy to work.

ANGOOD: Thank you. Great comments from all of you.

At some level, all physicians are leaders, and our association really strives to help the physician workforce and organizations as a whole embrace that sense of potential for physicians to provide stronger leadership.

Remember, leadership drives the culture in any organization, whether it's clinical or nonclinical. The culture of your organization knows when the leadership is working well or not. And physician leaders, physicians as a whole, are often closely tied into that culture; they drive the culture indirectly as well as directly. Physician leadership is pivotal.